REVERB

This book is a work of fiction. The names, characters, places and incidents are products of the author's imagination or have been used fictitiously and are not to be construed as real. Any resemblance to persons, living or dead, actual events, locales or organizations is entirely coincidental.

© 2018, 2019 Randolph Walker, Jr.
All rights reserved.

Image used courtesy of Jordy Torres Villalta

No part of this book may be reproduced in any form or by any electronic or mechanical means, including information storage and retrieval systems, without written permission from the author, except for the use of brief quotations in a book review.

ISBN: 9781020001017

45 Alternate Press, LLC
Hampton, VA

REVERB

The Adventures of Marz Banx

RAN WALKER

"My goal is to create something so dope my grandchildren will still be nodding their heads to it long after I'm gone."

— MARVIN "THE MARTIAN" EPPS

CHAPTER ONE

It was only while I was in the air, headed to Nashville, that it began to sink in that I was actually going through with all of this. After all, what the hell did I know about teaching?

Not a damn thing.

I've been an MC for as long as I can remember, and if it wasn't for Vandenheuval University wanting me to teach two courses on hip-hop music and culture, I would have just focused on my daughter's Sweet Sixteen. If everything went well, though, I would be able to let her know I'd be moving closer to her; that way we could spend more time together. That would be her *real* Sweet Sixteen gift, assuming there were no more flight hiccups and my duffle bag didn't wind up on the other side of the country once I landed.

Thankfully I and my luggage arrived together, leaving me just enough time to check into my hotel and run an iron over my suit before getting an Uber driver to take me over to the campus.

Vandenheuval University is one of those extremely well-endowed private schools for generationally wealthy white kids. Not really my thing.

When I was in high school I needed a school like Ellison-Wright College in Atlanta, a Historically Black College that was different than the racist public high school I'd gone to in Alabama. Even now, I'm not sure if I would be all that comfortable with my daughter going to a school like Vandenheuval when she graduates—even if her pops actually scored a job there.

They told me before I left Harlem that while this interview was largely a formality, it was still important that everything went well because there were still some people in the administration who were not 100% sold on having someone with my background going full-time at such a conservative institution.

Thankfully I arrived at the interview with a few minutes to spare, thus putting to bed the possibility of my tardiness as a direct result of my race.

Up until that moment, if you had asked me if I was nervous, I would have told you no. But by the time I realized how much I wanted—*needed*—this job, I started sweating like a Flavor Flav in a spelling bee. This was my shot at a new life—a chance to be closer to my daughter and push away from the New York hip-hop scene that allowed me to coast on my rent-controlled spot, while trying to fight off the pending gentrification that'll one day push me completely out of the city. It's a pretty embarrassing situation for someone who once had a gold-selling album, but the music industry is like a woman who fucks the shit out of you and then loses your number.

Carmen, my daughter's mother, has been cool

about my wrecked financials, mainly because she married some dude who plays for the Tennessee Titans, but I still feel like I could be doing so much more to pull my weight. My daughter deserves the best, and I'm hoping this job will give me the money, time, and proximity to make that happen. That's the plan anyway. That's why I'm sitting here waiting for the door just beyond the receptionist's desk to open.

The guy who emerges is an older white guy whose glistening, bald head reminds me of Destro from G.I. Joe. He looks at home in his gray wool three-piece suit. I look down at my Jordan 4s and for the first time wonder if I should have brought another pair of shoes for the interview—something a bit more formal.

"Mr. Banks," he says, eagerly extending his hand to meet mine. "It's a real honor."

I don't know if he's hamming it up, but I play along. "Good to meet you, too."

"Come on in," he says, ushering me into an office that, at a glance, looks much larger than my spot back in Harlem. He points to a plush antique chair in front of a massive mahogany desk. Rather than sit behind the desk, he pulls up a chair next to mine and faces me. He sits down and casually crosses his legs, one leg dangling over the other like a marble on the string of one of those perpetual motion toys. "Wow," he says, his smile so big and bright that he actually scares me for a moment. My conspiracy theory "self" whispers, *That's how they get you to drop your guard.*

Not wanting to seem rude, I say, "This is quite an office you have here."

"We try," he responds, his grin still fixed. "We definitely try here at Vandenheuval."

"I see." I nod my head like a broken bobblehead.

"You'll have to excuse me. I'm Theodore Butler, the dean of the School of Liberal Arts. Normally you would meet with the department chair for African-American Studies first. That's Dr. Nathan Delaney. But I insisted on talking with you first. I'm a huge fan!"

I look at this guy and think to myself that he *must* be lying, laying it on thick as a slice of Big Mama's hand-cut bologna, but then he mentions a song off of a mixtape I recorded long before I ever got signed. I look at him again and try to imagine this WASPy looking dude with a backward baseball cap, a hoodie, graffitied jeans, Uptowns, and a backpack—then I see it. *I see it!* This dude really *is* a fan.

I lean over and dap him up. At this, he's totally beside himself, geeked out 100%.

"We're just happy you're thinking about teaching —someone with your background, I mean. What is it? Two grammy nods? You were cheated on those. Well, anyway, let me tell you a little about Vandenheuval and what we're trying to do here."

For the next twenty minutes Theo, as he's told me to call him, does his damnedest to sell me on the university, as if the school's reputation didn't extend back into the 1800s, as if they didn't have an endowment of well over a billion dollars, as if there wasn't ivy literally growing on the side of the building, *as if slaves didn't build this motherfucker.*

The longer he talks, the more I realize the only way I won't walk away with this job is if I blow up the building on the way to the parking lot. He talks to me like I could, on command, sell out an arena like Jay Z. He doesn't need to know I can barely pack a small club or that I sit around praying for some film student shooting a hip-hop documentary to call me up to do an interview. Hell, I have no job to quit, just grinds to lay off.

Theo even goes so far as to say, "I just hope our offer is generous enough for you to seriously consider."

I play it cooler than the Good Humor Man. "I'm open," I respond.

After we finish up, he escorts me over to the department of African-American Studies, and it's there that he hands me off to Dr. Delaney, a short brother rocking a dashiki and a sports coat. This brother looks intense, and I can tell from my initial glance at him that Vandenheuval wanting to bring me here to teach was not his idea. He gives me one of those Uncle Ruckus/Sam Jackson-in-*Django Unchained*-kind of looks, the kind that says, "Boss, why you bringin' dis new nigga to da plantation?"

He shakes my hand firmly and guides me into his smaller, yet still impressive, office.

"How was your trip in, Mr. Banks?" he asks. The way he says "mister" smolders with disdain. It's the kind of title that is clearly not reciprocal since he has a PhD.

Normally I'm not fazed by these types of people. I'm one of the few MCs with a masters degree—quiet as kept—and would have probably gone for a PhD if my career hadn't taken off. But that was *years* ago. Still, I read a lot, and honestly, I don't think of myself as being an intellectual scrub next to this dude. At this point I'm more determined than ever to murk this interview—just to let this dude know exactly who he's fuckin' with.

"Not bad," I say.

"Coffee?"

"Nah. I'm good."

"Well, have a seat."

I sit down, and I'll be damned if this Negro doesn't fold his legs the exact same way as Theo. Must be some Vandenheuval shit, I guess.

"From looking at your resume, I see you have a masters degree in English. Can I ask if you've ever taught?"

"Nah. I've been a musician for the past twenty years."

"Oh?" he says, sounding surprised. "You play an instrument? I wasn't aware."

I can see right now he's one of those people who doesn't look at hip-hop as a real art form. I've had to deal with black folks shitting on my art for years, especially those early, lean years. But I keep my cool.

"Yeah, I play piano, trumpet, bass, drums, and a little guitar. But I prefer the lyrical dexterity and poetic possibilities afforded me by compositional structures that employ a sixteen bar framework."

Take that motherfucker.

"I see," he says. "Quite impressive."

"I guess. My moms was a classically trained pianist, my father a saxophonist, so music just runs in my family."

"Dr. Butler seems to feel you could offer a lot to this department. I've heard of other schools bringing on hip-hoppers to teach classes, but I'm curious to hear how you feel hip-hop merits the same discussion as, say, the Harlem Renaissance," he says, interlocking his fingers on his lap.

Hip-hoppers? Seriously?

I take a deep breath, as I consider the fact that this guy would be my primary obstacle to getting this job.

I need this. My Harlem life just doesn't work for me anymore. I can't keep having Jazz sleep on old beat up sofas when she comes to visit. My heart hurts that I can't do more for her. It's then that I realize that if Vandenheuval doesn't really want me, I'll just have to keep pushing on until I find another job opportunity in Nashville. I'd write country music if I had to.

But I'm not getting knocked out the box by this dude without a fight.

"I guess," I start, "when I think of the Harlem Renaissance, or the Black Arts Movement, for that matter, I think of the great poets, musicians, artists, and choreographers of the day. That's not that different from MCs, DJs, graffiti artists, and b-boys. Those four quadrants—plus some Knowledge—are the foundations for any artistic movement. Same thing.

"Langston. Sanchez. KRS1. They're all related. Voices of a culture in the macro sense, the culture of African Americans cultivating space in this land that so desperately wants to silence our voices.

"What do I bring? Experience. Experience from the frontlines of a culture that's gone more global than anything ever produced by any group of people that didn't have first-class citizenship. That's why I'm here.

"Make no mistake about this, Dr. Delaney. I'm *very* serious about this culture that I love."

He looks at me for a long moment, unable to say anything. He finally uncrosses his legs and stands up. "Well, Mr. Banks, I should probably introduce you to some of the other members of the department."

IF SOMEONE HAD TOLD me when I was a kid that I'd be trying to teach college students by the time I turned forty, I would have shrugged it off and said, "Whatever." I don't even think my parents would have pegged me for an educator.

My government name is Marzatrek Banks, but Pops called me Marz out the womb. In actuality, he wanted my government name to be Marz.

He figured me to be a Marz when I popped out all pork and beans. Moms wasn't too cool on the funky spelling of a planet as her only son's name, so she made up the name Marzatrek on the spot. (I guess if I was born a girl, she'd have called me Marzipan.)

Marzatrek Banks. Well, actually, Marzatrek David Banks. But I've been going by Marz for as long as I can remember. When I started MCing, I originally used the name Chocolate Milk—as in Milky Way. Yeah, I was a serious science nerd growing up. It wasn't until I was in college spitting at open mics that I realized my name was "spaced out" enough on its own. All I did was take away the "ks" and replace with an "x." Marz Banx is still phonetically the same, but the "x" indicates that unknown factor, that part of me, the music, the universe, that you can't readily explain.

Shortly after I started going by my new name, I met a cat named Marvin Epps, who was on the same shit as me. He went by the name Marvin the Martian, so it was like we were destined to be a rap group. That's how we became the Space Modulators. We were a weapon against all wack MCs, and frankly, we didn't give a shit if anyone got us. Tribe and Digable Planets had freed us up, imagination-wise, to explore hip-hop on our own terms.

When I told Pops and Moms I wanted to MC, they weren't really surprised. Actually they were supportive. It was that support that allowed me to follow Moms's recommendation that I consider doing a masters degree—just to have another weapon in my arsenal. She didn't sell it as a Plan B or some kind of fallback deal. She was like, "Doing a masters in English could give you more fuel for your rhymes, metaphors, and all that." She could have been running game on me, but she was right in the end. I seriously believe I'm a doper MC because of her advice. I have this ridiculous Cabinet of Curiosities when it comes to allusions and other obscure references.

I guess, in the end, the masters did give me an edge musically, but it's also offering me another chance at a very different life now. With the optimism from my Vandenheuval interviews still ringing in my head, I think my chances of getting an offer remain pretty high. Still, if things fall through, the experience of interviewing with a school like this lets me know I can hang with the folks in the Ivory Tower. I'm a quick study, so I can take what I learned from this experience and apply it to my next interview with another school. I'm committed to being closer to Jazz. She has two years before she graduates, and I want to make these years count even more than the rest.

I head back to my hotel to change. Jazz and Carmen aren't expecting me until tomorrow, so that leaves my evening open.

Sitting on the king-size bed in my room, I consider my options: get an Uber around the city or just rent a car and head over to my old stomping grounds in Memphis. I used to hook up with this sista over there when Marv and I passed through doing little shows here and there. I wonder what she's been up to. If I were on Facebook I'd know this shit already, but I'm a Twitter nut because, to me, that shit's a whole lot simpler. Hashtag this, link that, say some entertaining shit. Twitter was designed for an MC like me.

I pick up my phone and scroll through my contacts to see if I still have her number.

Noni. Noni. Noni.

And there it is. Her number, in all its glory. I dial it and she picks up.

"Marz?"

"Yeah, baby. What's up?"

"Shit. You in town?"

"Something like that. I'm here in Nashville. I might be coming over that way later tonight, though."

"For real? We should hook up."

I knew the shit wouldn't be difficult, but this was too fucking easy.

Still, with the years that've passed, I have no idea

of what she looks like now. It probably doesn't even matter anyway. Hell, I've put on a few pounds my damn self. A fuck is a fuck is a fuck, and since I gave up smoking, getting a piece of ass is harder to turn down, especially when it's being offered by someone who knows how to really put it down. Back in the day I used to call her my Bissell 'cause she could suck a nigga dry.

"That's what's up," I say. "You still at the same spot?"

"Nah. I'll send you the address. I gotta call around and get a babysitter for my son, though."

"You have a son? How old?"

"Don't worry, Marz. He ain't yours."

"That's not what I meant," I say, although that's exactly what I meant.

"He's nine. That boy is my heart."

"I feel you," I respond, still doing the math in my head and wiping my brow when I realize that she's right.

"Still, it's been a while since a sister's been broke off."

"I love that you are so direct."

"Marz, you know me. We go back. I don't fuck around. That's why you fuck with me."

I chuckle. She's so fucking gangsta—and I love that shit.

"I'm gonna go ahead and rent this car and head that way. Text me your info."

"Okay. Call me when you get to Memphis. That way I can make sure I'm back from dropping off Daquan."

"Mos def."

I hang up and within a minute her address comes through via text.

I grab a shower, head to the car rental place near the airport, and rent a mid-sized sedan.

Memphis, here I come.

CHAPTER TWO

I've never really been one for groupies. I just never viewed myself as the kind of dude women would throw their drawz at. I'm just a regular-looking dude with a gap between his front teeth and an off-again-on-again beard.

I don't think of Noni as a groupie, though. We're actually cool. Granted, she did come out to one of my shows—which is how I met her—and came up to me after we had just performed. I didn't sweat her; she didn't sweat me. We just started talking about music we listened to growing up, while splitting a plate of wings. Yeah, she was sexy, but she wasn't the only sexy woman at the club that night. She was just the coolest.

After a few hours of shooting the shit, she offered me a place to sleep for the night. We went back to her crib and found out we were compatible in more ways than one. Stevie has this song "I Was Made to Love Her." Well, after a few hours of hardcore banging, I could have written a song like that, switching out the "love" part with something a bit more graphic. We were just good together. When we finished, we would dap each other like boys and watch Sports Center.

Before I left her crib that first time, we vowed we would connect the next time either of us passed through the other's city. Because I was now living in Harlem, all our hook-ups came when I passed through Memphis, usually every year or so until we kind of faded out. I didn't know if the standing invitation was still in effect until I called her.

Truthfully, the biggest part of my fading out with Noni had to do with me trying to get my shit straight with Carmen, before and after we had Jazz. But I had a problem with being with just one woman. I've often questioned if I'm just not wired to be monogamous.

Carmen couldn't deal with me and my shit, so she moved my daughter with her down to Nashville. That move broke my heart into a million pieces. I even went so far as to propose to her, after apologizing my ass off. She turned me down, and for a while I explored my legal options on custody. That was my emotions talking, though. My lifestyle was so all over the place. I was in no place to raise a girl by myself. Shit only really got smoothed out when Carmen started dating that football player from the Titans. By that time, we had completely settled into our roles. I would come visit Jazz or have her for a few weeks in the summer.

Just seeing what Carmen was doing in terms of raising our daughter made me fall in love with her all over again. But our time had passed. I wanted her to be happy, so I left her to build a new life with ol' boy.

After that, I just kept a pretty low profile, not really dating too much. The only reason I bothered Noni is because we have some pretty good history with each other.

By the time I reach the Germantown area off I-40, I pick up my phone and call her. She answers on the second ring.

"I'm just getting to Memphis."

"A'ight. You need directions?"

"I'm good with your text and the GPS."

"Well, I'll see you in a few. Be safe."

"Will do," I say and hang up.

I have already told myself that, even if we don't hook up, we can still hang and catch up on old times, maybe watch a game on TV.

The GPS leads me down around the Memphis International Airport and dumps me off on a road that runs right through the hood. I can tell by my phone's GPS that this is her neighborhood. I shake my head.

The last time I came to see her, she was living off Poplar Avenue, a few blocks from the Beale Street tourist area. It wasn't the Ritz Carlton, but it wasn't straight hood either. I know from my own experience that you have to do the best you can with housing. Some people might call my neighborhood in Harlem rough, since the gentrification hasn't yet worked its way all the way over to us. Plus, I don't even own my own shit, so I'm damn sure not knocking anyone else. Still, I'm on high alert.

I park my car near a light pole and pat myself on the back for getting insurance with the rental. I don't have any valuables in the car, so I lock up and walk the stairs to the second floor of what is clearly Hood

Central. I don't have to look farther than all the activity outside to know section 8 is deep in this bitch.

I knock on the door, and I hear the jiggling of multiple locks. A shadow shifts behind the keyhole, and while I'm in plain view, I hear Noni say, "Who's there?"

"Me. Marz."

The door cracks open just enough for me to ease through. The lights are dim and the smell of lit wild raspberry candles is heavy in the air. Noni is already in her lingerie and is not playing at all. She's a little thicker than I remember, but the extra weight is in all the right places. Her hips are fuller, her legs thicker and more toned, and she's gone natural with this stunning curly Afro. In short, she looks even sexier than she did the last time I saw her.

"Damn," I say, my mouth falling open. The mental scenario I conjured up on the drive over was that we would talk a little and see if we could build back up to where we were years ago.

"Don't start getting all brand new on me," she says. "We're not strangers."

In that moment my mind flashes back to the visual of her back arched, her legs wide, as I enter her from behind, her weave sticking to the sweat on her back. I feel the thickening of my crotch and the throbbing of wanting to enter her again, this new and improved Noni.

"Come on back," she says, taking me lightly by the fingertips, as if guiding someone who already knows the way to the destination.

We enter a rather large room, and her king-size bed looks almost majestic with the sheer canopy hanging down from above. The candles I smelled when I came in are lined along both sides of the room on dressers and desks, spaced out so as to not make any single area too bright. Classic Jodeci is playing in the background—and she's standing there, one hand on her hip, the other on her thigh looking like the queen of Wakanda, and all I want to do is yank off my clothes in a single motion, as if all of my shit has been sewn together like a clown suit.

She then proceeds to do a Looney Tune/Steinbeck *Of Mice and Men* on me: "I will suck him and fuck him and call him George!" And it's all good, cozy like a quilt your grandmother sewed for you as a baby. Ass rising and falling like the tail of a humpback whale. Oh Noni.

We collapse onto the bed, the sheets wet with sweat and sex—and that lingering scent of wax and wild raspberry rounding out the cocktail. We shower and go at it again, but when we come out of the bathroom, there's a surprise.

This thug-ass nigga is standing in the middle of the room, all screw-faced. His hands are balled up like anvils.

Oh shit! So this is how I'm gonna die. Forty years old, and it all ends here in these projects, I think, realizing that I'm too vulnerable to do anything at this point.

I muster up my Stringer Bell, knowing the end is imminent and start to say, "Well, get on with it!"—but I don't. Instead, I reach for a towel that's not there.

"What the fuck?" ol' boy says.

"You made a copy of the key?" Noni responds.

"My son, my motherfucking key. Where is my son while you all up in here fucking around like a two-dollar chicken."

"He at Miss Shirley's."

This entire conversation is happening while Noni and I are buck naked, and this nigga is talking to her like fucking Jerry Maguire standing in the shower room acting like wet ass ain't all up in the spot.

"And this motherfucker," he says, pointing at me. "Hold up! Oh shit!"

I'm ready to run full-speed at him and jump out the window if need be.

"Yo, you Marz Banx!" he says.

I don't know what to do, so I nod.

"I'm a big fan. You and Marv, man! I got all y'alls shit!" he says, covering his mouth and placing one hand on his knee in disbelief.

"Thanks?" I offer.

He then turns to Noni, whose naked body is still glistening in the light of the candles. "You fuckin' with Marz Banx? Ha! That's fucking bananas!" Then he turns back to me. "Yo, can I get a pic with you for my Instagram?"

I can't believe my ears. But it slowly dawns on me that he's not going to kill me. "No problem," I say, relieved. "Let me put on my clothes first."

"Sure. Here," he says, handing me a pile of clothes at the foot of the bodussy-soaked bed.

Now I've seen everything. Stick a fork in me. I'm officially done.

I take the pic with this nigga, hug Noni goodbye, and hop in my rental, headed back to Nashville, too dazed to replay any of the craziness that just happened.

Peace out, Memphis.

CHAPTER THREE

On the drive home, while listening to Bobby Womack's "If You Think You're Lonely Now" on the radio, I replay everything that happened only moments earlier. Ol' boy didn't really get as hostile as I would have expected. With him being her baby's daddy, he didn't seem to have any real sense of attachment to her, which could only mean one of two things: either he was completely over her sexually and had moved on or Noni was so good in bed that he'd actually wait his turn. At this point, though, I couldn't care less. I'm alive, safe, and headed back to my quiet room at the Holiday Inn Express. And Noni, well she was cooler than the other side of the pillow, completely unshook by dude's shenanigans.

As I continue driving, I flip Womack's words around and realize that I'm probably the lonely one. I'm forty, have never been married, and am a few miles away from being Father of the Year to a beautiful soon-to-be-sixteen-year-old, who reminds me so much of Moms. I've got to do better. At the rate

I'm going I'll have no one in my life willing to help me in and out of my Depends.

It's not that I've never been in love before. It's just that I've never felt so strongly for a woman that it muted my desire to be with other women. I have known this about myself ever since my escapades in high school and have never tried to hide this from any of the women I've dated. How Carmen and I were able to last the three years we did is that she turned a blind eye to all of my shit and took the S.O.S. Band route (*I don't care about your other girls. Just be good to me.*) That shit works okay until you have a child together. I can't blame her not wanting Jazz growing up in an environment like that.

I even offered to change so Carmen and Jazz would stay, but she knew me well enough to know that I was likely to fall back to my normal routine once the scare of them leaving was no longer there.

Roughly twenty-five miles out from Nashville, the radio station actually starts playing one of my songs; well, technically it's one of Tangela Dawn's songs, but I have sixteen bars on the track and get songwriting royalties off of it, so in that regard, it's one of my songs, too. These days Tangela is known primarily for acting in big budget movies, but before that she was a singer—and before *that* she was an MC doing guest verses on the Space Modulator albums. Back then she went by T. Swift, a name lost on anyone who wasn't a die-hard sci-fi buff. T. Swift as in Thomas A. Swift, a character whose name forms the TAS in the acronym TASER (the remaining letters meaning "Electronic Rifle"). With Space Modulator's name coming from a fictional weapon used by Marvin the Martian, Tangela's flavor was right in line with our approach. I think the term they use now for our style of music is *Afrofuturism*. Back then, though, we were just some kids spitting about the shit we loved.

But once Tangela did a few hooks alongside her sixteen and thirty-two bar drops, it became clear to anyone who was paying attention that she had pipes and that her career would move into an entirely different direction with the right management and production—and that's what happened.

It's been roughly two years since I've spoken to her, but we're still cool. Of course she can't go anywhere without being mobbed. Me, on the other hand, I can go days without anyone coming up to me. Now since I got spotted by Noni's baby's daddy, I probably won't get stopped again for a few days. Even to Jazz I'm just her pops, who happens to have a few famous friends.

Originally, it had been my plan to DJ her sweet sixteen (a gig I normally charge a few grand for in New York), but she was worried my tastes were too old school.

"Daddy, no offense, but no one really listens to your type of music anymore."

"Yeah they do," I responded. "That 'My Boo' song by Ghost Town DJs dropped twenty years ago—same as my stuff. The only difference is that the Running Man dance back then required athletic coordination, while this new thing you guys call 'The Running Man' looks like someone debating whether or not they want to go to the restroom."

"Oh Daddy!"

"Tell me I'm lying."

She only laughed.

Her laughter softened me up a bit and she told me about the Korean-American DJ Optimus Rhyme who her stepdad, Derrick, had already hired, a kid who would be DJing from his laptop. If that's what Jazz wanted, so be it. I just want her to be happy.

So in two days I will be wearing only one hat at her party: father.

By the time I park outside the hotel I am so tired that I am relieved my room is on the first floor. I crash as soon as my face touches the pillow, the dry funk of nostalgic sex the only blanket I need.

CHAPTER FOUR

Jasmine Lashelle Banks was born four weeks early due to complications with Carmen's pregnancy. She was delivered via Caesarian section and spent four weeks on breathing tubes in an incubation isolette, her small, fragile body clinging to life each day. I had never experienced anything so scary in my life. I can only imagine what Carmen was going through.

She and I went several times every day to sit with Jazz, holding her beneath our shirts against our bare skin, loving her to full health. After two weeks the NICU nurses no longer had to feed her through the thin tube they had running through her nose down into her stomach. She grew and by the time she turned one, she was nearly the same size, weight, and mental development as kids born on time. Other than a small touch of asthma, there is nothing about our daughter that would suggest she was a preemie.

Carmen and I were blessed—and we know this, which is why both of us still actively support the

March of Dimes. Jazz jokes that the 5K Carmen and I do each year to raise money is the only time our parental behaviors align. We just nod and smile. There is one more area where Carmen and I are similar: we both shower Jazz with affection. In my mind I will never be able to make up for all of the hugs and kisses I missed out on while she was in that NICU isolette, and the way I see it, she'll just have to accept my ongoing affections as the price of being my daughter.

Now she's turning sixteen. Where has all of that time gone? I remember holding her, while she slept in my arms. I remember her hating the idea of sleeping on her back and Carmen and I being afraid of the stuff we were hearing about Sudden Infant Death Syndrome. We had fought so hard to bring her home from the hospital that running the risk of having her sleep in the wrong position was not an option.

And, lord, the reflux! Walking around the kitchen while she cried at three o'clock in the morning, as we tried to figure out what we could possibility do to ease her discomfort.

All of that was almost sixteen years ago.

On a professional level, though, in those sixteen years I've released five LPs, two mixtapes, a solo project, and countless guest spots on other people's joints. I never caught on with the mainstream enough to be set for life. Never had that cross-over hit or video. Guess that makes me "hood" famous. That DJ Optimus Rhyme—I looked him up—has two free mixtapes only available as downloads and he is far more famous than I am.

The Internet is a motherfucker.

I wake up early and head downstairs to grab my complimentary breakfast of powdered eggs, cereal, and coffee. I glance at my phone and see a text from Noni, thanking me for last night. I respond with some similar shit, then put my phone down to finish eating.

I wonder if Jazz is awake and decide to call her. She picks up on the fourth ring.

"Daddy," she says, her voice filled with sleep. "Are you in town yet?"

"I'm here, baby girl. I checked in last night."

"Cool. Can't wait to see you."

"You have plans for lunch?" I ask.

"Not really."

"Wanna grab a bite with your old man?"

"Yeah. About what time?"

"Whenever you want."

I can hear her yawning and stretching, and I'm reminded of the way she stretched her arms right after she was born.

"Can you meet me at noon over here?" she says.

"I'll be there."

She stretches and yawns again.

"Well, I'll let you get up and get situated," I say.

"Okay, Daddy. See you at noon. Love you."

"Love you, too."

I hang up the phone feeling good in the way only a proud parent can.

Glancing at my watch, I see that I have just

under four hours to check on Jazz's gift before I go to pick her up.

Originally my plan was to DJ her Sweet Sixteen, but Derrick changed all of that. That left me feeling a little disappointed, but I shook it off and turned to Plan B.

I pick up my phone and call Laird, the guy helping me with Jazz's gift.

"How's it coming?" I ask after we exchange greetings.

"Just about done. You can roll through around five today, and everything should be ready," Laird says.

"A'ight. Peace," I respond, hanging up.

Laird is my dude from way back and probably one of the few people I know, besides Carmen, who transplanted to the Nashville metro area from New York City. I used to joke with him about moving down South.

"I didn't know country musicians wore grills."

He laughed it off, because apparently he knew something about Tennesseans that I didn't know—even now—because he's been running a successful business here for at least a decade.

Back in the day when backpack rappers wanted to get a little light jewelry to up our game, we went to Laird. Alex Laird's red hair and beard made him stand out in New York. Dude could have been a Viking or a Wildling from *Game of Thrones*, if you didn't already know him as a jeweler. Diddy and those dudes went to Jacob's, but dudes like me, who weren't all about trying to screen blood diamonds from the rest, went with a guy who worked primarily in gold and non-conflict stones. I'm still baffled that he moved to Nashville, though. He was NYC through and through. But word on the street is that he fell in love with a country girl and moved south to be closer to her family once they started having kids.

I can't blame him.

It took me nearly sixteen years, but now I can't imagine being away from my daughter any longer. Having both of her parents nearby has to be a plus. I owe her that much since I was fortunate enough to have Moms and Pops there for me when I was coming up.

I CHECK my phone and find a record shop downtown. I figure I'll go through and peep the vinyls before I head over to scoop up Jazz. Its' kind of hard being an MC who came up in the 90s and not be a vinyl hunter. And I'm pretty old school with my collecting. I like walking into an actual shop and combing through the vinyls, whether it's Amoeba in San Fran or Plan 9 in Richmond, Virginia. I know I could easily get on the Internet and find stuff, but I'm really about the hunt. Plus, you never know what you'll come across. It could be a liner note across the bottom of the back cover or a dope image on the front that makes me pause and consider a record. I don't have enough fingers to count the number of samples we found that way back in the early days. Marv was especially good at combing the creates.

But no one had Dilla beat. When he sampled that Samba joint "Sandade Vem Correndo" by Stan

Getz and Luiz Bonfá at two minutes and three seconds in, creating the legendary beat for Pharcyde's "Runnin'," there was no question who the real beat king was. Marv was a distant second to Dilla, but to even be in Dilla's universe was an accomplishment unto itself.

By the time I arrive at Ben's Records (no imagination on the name), I'm eager to see what a store in Nashville might carry. After a little over an hour, I come away with some old Leon Russell, a little Ray Charles, and an album by Little Milton. My tastes in music have always been diverse, and from years of writing and performing, I'd say they've grown even more eclectic over the years.

When I place the records in my satchel on the backseat of the rental, I take a moment to remember Marv. It's times like this when I really miss him—when the realization that there'll never be another Space Modulator album really sinks in. When I slip into this melancholy funk, I'm relieved only by the fact that I'd spoken with him the week before he died in a car crash and we'd cleared the air between us. We had even talked about getting back together and recording one more joint for the fans.

That was over five years ago.

I didn't stop rhyming, but my need to be in the studio fell off. Even my solo joints felt too fucking pop. The label wanted me to do all this shit that just wasn't me, so I stepped away to do my own thing at my own speed. Now I just drop joints on SoundCloud from time to time and focus on DJing, a skill I had to develop after years of doing nothing but MCing. I'm really trying to build up my name there, but there are already so many other celebrity DJs.

Still, I do get to spin from time to time (just not at my own daughter's Sweet Sixteen).

If this teaching job comes through, though, a lot of my concerns will be in the rearview. A steady paycheck. A chance to teach about something I love. That's what awaits me on a professional tip if Vandenheuval still wants to fuck with me.

CHAPTER FIVE

When I was thirteen and in the eighth grade, I witnessed my first MC battle. Before that, anyone interested in rapping wrote rhymes in a notebook and kept them personal. Growing up in a small town in Alabama, we never got the hot shit when it first dropped. This was in the days before the Internet. It was always someone who went "up North" in the summer and came back with the list of what was hot. These dudes were our tastemakers, and this particular summer they brought back two big things: New Jack Swing and MC battles. While the two seem disparate on the surface, they actually worked together to elevate the music game in my hometown.

New Jack Swing, largely built on the intricate percussion programming and keyboarding of Teddy Riley, pushed a whole new style of dance to the forefront. With the more athletic dance moves came the dance partners—usually you would partner on some Kid 'N Play-style shit. Because you now had dance partners (this was before the return of the Southern b-boy crews), you inevitably found yourself in two-on-two dance floor battles that could erupt anywhere from behind the bleachers during the Friday night football game to the back of the classroom whenever a teacher stepped out for a smoke.

Once the foundation had been laid for public battling, all it took was a few dope beatboxers, the inclination to rap, and a crowd and it was on!

At first MC battling consisted of people writing down rhymes, memorizing them, and finding the right person to battle so you could spit that shit and make it fresh. But it didn't take long for that approach to get stale. If you were a hip-hop head, you could spot a memorized diss a mile away. That forced the few of us who were committed to the mic to start training ourselves to freestyle.

In high school I was just okay when it came to freestyling, mainly because I was afraid of saying shit that might make me sound like a nerd. But by the time I got to Ellison-Wright College, I had already said, "Fuck it." By that time, I had come to accept the fact that being well-read was a plus when it came to MCing.

Reading a lot of classic poetry helped me to learn about slant rhymes and assonance. That was my tool for keeping a cypher going. If you only rhyme words that are pure rhymes, you'll find yourself saying a lot of the same shit over and over. With slant rhymes, you intone to get a similar sound and that gives you a lot of space to be creative. I could do more sci-fi references since a lot of those words are made up and don't exactly rhyme with everyday words. This was back when I was still Chocolate Milk. But I was starting to build up my rep.

I remember one time battling this other dude in college who was an engineering major rhyming under the name MC Squared. We went bar for bar and I swear I ate through all of my "go-to" rhymes and had to completely push myself into a new spatial abyss of MCing. It was that day that I discovered how my deep my shit really ran, how real MCing was in my soul. I felt like I could have rhymed for hours. After that, I became that MC in the cypher that dudes expected to take it to some André 3000 shit. And that's when Marv and I hooked up.

If you had told me that we would carve out our own little planet in the galaxy of Hip-Hop, I might've laughed you off. We were living for the next beat, the next rhyme, the next chance at being immortal on wax.

A MASSIVE TEXT message fills my phone, and I wonder how a person could compose something like this at great length using only their thumbs. It's from Caldwell, my former manager.

He starts with a short greeting and then launches into how *Slay 'Em* magazine has listed me in their top 25 MCs of all time and how people still want to work with me and how it might be time for me to give some more thought to my rap career. My head is spinning by the time I make it through the message. Why he didn't call me with this so he could parse out all of the info without overwhelming me is a whole other issue. Caldwell is one of those dudes who believes everything needs to have a paper (or digital) trail, even matters bordering on personal. He definitely couldn't run for president—but he'd probably make a decent lawyer.

I read the text again. And again.

The fact that I might be able to give a boost to my rap career is appealing in so many ways. Top 25? Of all time? I comb through the hundreds of MCs I know and marvel that the top rap magazine in the game has put me on their hip-hop Mount Rushmore. Rap doesn't have a Hall of Fame—but if it did, it's likely the voters would come largely from the editorial staff over at *Slay 'Em*.

There's a bittersweet pang underneath it all, though. While I don't know for absolute sure, I feel if Caldwell knew Marv made the list, he would've said so. His M.O. back before I did my solo shit was to always try to market the two of us together. "There's a mystique that comes with a group that's just not there with solo acts," he would say. Then he'd add that Q-Tip and André 3000 are even that much more elevated because they came from dope groups that capitalized on contrasting their rhyme styles with those of the other members in their group. But even with Caldwell's analogy it was clear that one MC got more shine than the other, with no disrespect to the late great Phife Dawg and the legendary Big Boi.

Like Dilla, Marv was a legendary beat maker who got most of his love for that and not his rhymes—which were also dope. Kanye avoided that fate by rhyming through the wires in his jaws and financing his own music video. Q-Tip is probably one of the bigger MCs to ever be his own group's primary beat maker. Could Marv have been another Q-Tip?

Asking "what if" questions is pretty pointless now, though.

I wish Marv were still around for me to tell the news to. He was never the jealous type. He was also not the kind of dude who was insecure about his shit. We didn't compete like spoiled kids trying to one-up the other. We played Space Modulator like a team. Sometimes my role was to play offense, other times defense.

When I consider the other parts of Caldwell's text about possible future collabs with the new school dudes, I go ahead and call him back.

"Marz, my man," he answers. "Long time, no hear."

"You know how it is. You still in the business?"

"Working with a few cats here and there. I'm pretty much trying to get a handle on the real estate game now."

"Caldwell Stone is selling houses?" I say, trying to imagine a guy who owns over two hundred different pairs of Air Force Ones wearing a suit and tie.

"Nah. I'm doing time shares and stuff. It's going all right, too. You interested? I could send you some info—and maybe a few coupons to activities in the area."

"I'm good. I'm trying to keep my focus on moving to Nashville."

"Well," Caldwell says. I can hear the smile in his voice. "Moving closer to Jazz. Can't knock you for that. She's a wonderful little girl."

"She turns sixteen tomorrow."

"Damn. They really grow up fast, don't they?"

"Man, who you telling?"

We continue on for another minute catching up with small talk when Caldwell says, "So that's some incredible news on that *Slay 'Em* list, huh? But then again, they're just confirming what I've always known."

"'Thanks."

"I couldn't have worked with you and Marv for all them years if I didn't think you guys had it, n'ah mean?'

"Respect," I say.

"I'm just telling the truth. And from the way my phone's been blown' up, you hotter than fish grease right now, son. Everybody wants to fuck with you. These young 'uns offering twenty grand for sixteen bars. That's just spitting on the track. We aint even talkin' 'bout videos and appearances and shit. Apparently you just about everybody's inspiration—or so they say. Hell, the way shit is going, I keep half-expecting the Rock & Roll Hall of Fame in Cleveland to call telling me you boys got in."

Caldwell is gassing me up so hard I'm not able to separate the truth from the hyperbole. But at the end of the day, hip-hop is about showing and proving, so if my stock is suddenly going through the roof, I need to see something. Hell, anything.

"You see what you can shake loose," I say. "But know this: I plan to make Nashville my home, so dudes need to factor that shit in, plane tickets and all. I want to see something for real jump off, but just know that my girl comes first. Real talk."

"I feel you. Let's holler next week and I should have something more for you then."

"Bet."

"A'ight, Marz. Give Jazz a hug for me."
"Will do."
"Peace."

CHAPTER SIX

Carmen and Jazz live in this swanky neighborhood, the kind of place you'd expect a professional athlete to purchase a house. Not really being big on pro football, especially since I grew up in a town so small we didn't even have a minor league baseball team within three hours of us, I don't know if Derrick even starts or what position he plays. He's a good enough guy, though. He treats Carmen and Jazz well, as far as I can tell, and even claims to have copped several of my joints back in the day.

I park my rental sedan in their winding driveway, but Jazz runs up to me and grabs me in one of her warm embraces before I can reach the doorbell.

"Daddy!" She squeezes me hard, and I feel a lump in my throat as I hold her in my arms. It feels like yesterday when I had her under my shirt, against my chest, trying to do everything we could to take her home from NICU. I guess she will always be my baby girl.

"Jazz," I respond, lifting her off the ground and spinning her in a circle.

As I take her in, I'm still amazed at how much she grows between our visits. She looks like a beautiful young woman. Before she was born, Carmen and I would make up games about who Jazz would look like the most. Whose idiosyncrasies she would take on. Whose personality she would most likely resemble. We wondered what her voice would sound like. But in the end, all of that didn't really matter. It was just something to do to channel our excitement about having a child. I would have loved her madly if there was nothing of hers that resembled me. As it would turn out, though, she looks a lot like me. Same complexion. Same eyes. Same round face. It's obvious to anyone paying attention that she's my daughter. Pops used to joke that if a baby came out looking like her daddy, that meant the daddy had really put some good dick on the mommy. He would say this with a sly smile, but ironically, I don't see much resemblance between him and me. I guess at the end of the day we see what we want to see.

"Your mama around?" I ask. "Just wanted to say hello before we dipped out."

"She and Derrick are out running errands for tomorrow."

"It's a big day. You excited?"

"Kind of." The words sort of tumble out in this resignation of apathy or maybe even melancholy. It kills me to hear my baby girl is anything but enthused over her Sweet Sixteen.

"Talk to me."

"I'm just like whatever. Three girls have had Sweet Sixteens—big MTV-style ones—and I'm just starting to feel like it's all so extra."

"You're turning sixteen—not twenty-five. You're

supposed to want to ball out and all that stuff. You got Optimus Rhyme doing the party."

She sighs. "To tell you the truth, I didn't even want to have a party."

"Don't talk like that. You're breaking my heart."

"No, Daddy, I'm serious. Mom and Derrick wanted me to have all of this. I'm just being a good sport."

"I tell you what," I say. "Let's go grab a bite and you can tell me about how you really want to celebrate your birthday. Is that cool?"

Her face softens and I see the beginning of a smile forming in the corners of her mouth. "Sure."

Jazz tells me about a soul food shack across town, and we're there within twenty minutes. The neighborhood reminds me of all the neighborhoods I've seen from Memphis to Harlem: former capitals of the black middle class, now struggling against deterioration, fighting that last battle against the inevitability of gentrification. A year from now this place will either be gone to Soul Food Heaven or coopted by Becky and Blair as a place to frequent when they want to sample the adventurous (sodium and sugar-infused) goodies of the Southern Negro. I could freestyle all day long about this shit if I wanted.

Even though I'm at home here, I still check to make sure I didn't leave anything on the car seats before I lock that motherfucker up. I love my people, but I ain't a damn fool.

We cop a booth off to the side, beneath a signed

picture of the late, great Maurice White, one of the few true musical geniuses of the twentieth century, if you ask me.

Jazz points to it before resting her hands on the dinged up wooden table in front of us. "Thought you'd like this," she says, smiling.

I smile back. "You already know that."

I reach out and take her hands in mine, remembering for a second her gripping my finger, as I extended one of my hands through a hole in her NICU isolette. We have come a long way, the two of us.

The place is moderately packed with other black people. There is one stray white couple tucked away at a booth in the back, the designated brave souls looking to "Columbus" this spot for upcoming Yuppies.

"You come here a lot?" I ask, grabbing one of the thin paper menus—single page, front and back—and perusing the offerings.

"Maybe like once a month with one of my girls. She likes doing the open mic night. The food is pretty good, though."

"Hope your girl is coming through tomorrow. I'd like to meet anyone keeping a poetic influence around my baby girl."

She laughs. "Yeah, LaTasha will be there."

"Cool."

A server wearing the name tag "Pam Pam" approaches the table with two Mason jars of water.

"How y'all doin'?" Pam Pam says.

"Fantastic," I say. "And you?"

"Chile, blessed and highly favored!"

For a moment I thought she said highly flavored,

and now I find myself struggling not to imagine her thick nutmeg-colored body covered in whip cream. Oh Noni!

"Need more time to look over your menus?" she asks.

Jazz looks at me. "I'm ready. You?"

"How about you order me whatever my daughter is having," I tell Pam Pam.

"Sure thing, honey," she responds, before looking at my daughter and saying, "Girl, I love that hairstyle! What's yo curl pattern? 4B?"

"4C," Jazz says.

"I got 4C, too. You got to give me some pointers on this. I only been natural a year and I'm starting to crave that creamy crack again. I just don't know what to do with this sometimes, so I just keep it under a wrap."

Jazz nods. "It takes time to get used to it. Have you tried apple cider vinegar..."

I clear my throat before Pam Pam decides to put down her order tablet and have a full-blown discourse about hair care while my stomach growls. Plus, all this talk about what food or condiment they're putting in their hair is making me hungrier.

"You hear that?" Pam Pam says.

And as if one cue, Jazz says, "Yeah. Sounds a lot like a male ego."

They both look at me and smile.

After Jazz and I finish the hard-fried lemon pepper chicken wings and seasoned potato wedges, along with the fruit-infused sweet tea—compliments of Pam Pam ("my name is so nice you have to say it twice")—Jazz begins to open up to me about her birthday concerns.

The long and convoluted story my daughter tells me covers everything from a fall out with some of her associates because she took up for a girl being bullied for the way she dressed, to a boyfriend she caught cheating on her when she went through his phone and found a Snapchat screen shot of a where a girl had sexted him all of her business. Then there are the concerns Jazz has about Carmen and Derrick's relationship. "Derrick's phone gets him into as much trouble as my ex's." By the time she finishes, I'm astounded at how complicated my daughter's life is.

I offer words of comfort and encouragement, but I'm floored at how grown up she is, not just in terms of the situations she has to confront daily, but the manner in which she addresses them. As for what she says about Carmen and Derrick, I tell her that marriage is always a work in progress (from what I've heard) and that adults go through ups and downs in their relationships, but love usually wins out in the end. I know I'm blowing a little smoke here, but she's only sixteen. There's no point in fracturing what's left of her childhood innocence.

I'm tempted to tell her right then that I'm planning to move to Nashville, but I want that to be part of my surprise for tomorrow so I hold back.

"Excuse me, sir," the white guy from the back of the restaurant says as he stands over our table. "Are you Marz Banx?"

I look at Jazz and she smiles and nods.

"Yeah. What's good?" I say, dapping his extended hand.

"Oh my god! I have all of your music—the Space Modulator stuff, the SoundCloud mixes. I'm a true fan."

"Respect," I say, taking in the adoration. It's not often these days that people recognize me out and about (except at Noni's).

"Hey, can I get a pic?" he asks, handing his smart phone to his girl. She takes it eagerly.

She snaps a few pics in rapid succession and he thanks me like I found a cure for some disease ailing his mother.

When he leaves I settle back into my seat.

"Does it ever get old?" Jazz asks, smiling.

"These days? No. I'm not really famous. I'm more like a person who might have been slightly popular a while ago. My fans are far and few."

"I can tell you clearly don't read anything on social media. Right before you came over, someone tweeted you made some greatest MC of all time list."

"You saw that?"

"You're my dad. Of course I saw it—and retweeted it, too."

Hearing the approval in her voice makes it all worth it. Fathers should be proud of their daughters, but the reverse is kind of cool, too.

CHAPTER SEVEN

The first time I recorded a song was my junior year in college. Back then Marv was that producer dude in the dorm. He had a TR-808 drum machine, a mic and a wind guard made out of an old pair of pantyhose and a contorted wire hanger. The "booth" was a closet filled with stapled cardboard egg crates and McDonald's cup holders. None of that shit mattered, though, because the finished recording sounded pretty close to what we were hearing on the radio.

Once we had put together eight songs, we made a cassette, labeled it an album, and went for a drive in my old beat-up Dodge Dynasty, blasting the hell out of our shit through what was left of the factory Bose system. We were going to be famous.

I filled up notebook after notebook with rhymes, while Marv kept churning out dope beats. None of the dudes at Ellison-Wright College could fuck with us, so we took our act off-campus to local open mics at the Underground and any place where hungry MCs went to get seen by Jermaine Dupree, Dallas Austin, or Puffy.

We were ready and would stop at nothing to get a bonafide deal.

Marv's father was a copyright attorney so he instilled the fear of God into Marv about sampling other folk's music. "If you can't get it cleared yourself, make your label clear it—but whatever you do, don't use even a *second* of someone else's stuff without permission." We listened to him and as a result, we were one of the only groups that didn't do mixtapes of us freestyling over someone else's beats. Occasionally, Marv would sample something, reverse it, and camouflage it under a beat and we'd get away with it, but for the most part, the label we eventually signed to (Beast Mode Dynamite) cleared the samples we chose to use or Marv's pops would do it for us pro bono and pay the fee as a gift.

We were lucky to have Marv's pops around schooling us on copyright law. He broke down for us what music publishing was and how important it was to have some ownership in your songwriting. If it wasn't for him, we couldn't have done music full-time. I would have been teaching English at some middle school and rapping after work or during my vacation break.

In retrospect, Marv's pops was the first person in our families to understand just how far we could take this thing. It really is a damn shame that I haven't spoken to him since Marv's funeral. I guess it's been difficult for both of us. I mean, Marv's death was so sudden that I wish I could rewind time to keep him from falling asleep behind the wheel. I occasionally look at my phone and want to call him, but then reality sinks in, and I realize that our chapter together has passed—at least for now.

After we pull up to the house, Jazz pleads for me to come in, telling me she has something to give me. I've been in their house a few times, but as a general rule, I try not to loaf around there, interrupting the flow of whatever they've created as a family. But if my daughter wants me to come in, then I'm going in.

I follow her through the door, up the winding staircase to her room. I swear every time I see how huge her room is I feel both happy for her and sad for my damn self. My own daughter's room is twice the size of my room in Harlem. At least I know Derrick and Carmen are giving her what she deserves since I haven't been able to.

"Okay," she says, standing in front of a massive white bookshelf. "The last time I was at your crib in Harlem, I noticed the conspicuous absence of black women writers on your shelves."

I smile. This is the beautiful monster I have created with all these years of visiting bookstores and libraries with her. I try to plead my case, though. "I have some Toni Morrison and some Gloria Naylor in my stash, so don't even go there."

"Yeah and they are definitely royalty, but Dad, you have to read some black women who have written books in the new millennium. I picked up some books for you to take back with you. You have to read them, okay? They're really good. Plus, I want you to stay up on black women writers so you can understand their influences on my own work."

I smile. "So how's your novel coming?"

I love that I can ask my sixteen-year-old

daughter that question. Chris Rock once said a father's only job in life was to keep his daughter "off the pole." Well, writing a novel is definitely a hell of a long way from the pole.

"It comes in spurts, but sometimes I start making some real progress before I run out of steam."

"You need me to take a look at it for you?"

"It's not ready yet. I still have to work on it a little more before I can let you see it."

I nod. "Fair enough."

Jazz starts pulling books from her shelves, almost at random. She forms them into a stack in her hands and gently places them on the dresser beside me. "These are for you to read when you're out on tour."

"Who says I'm going on tour?" I say.

"Whatever, Mr. Greatest MC. Just make sure you keep these with you. I want you to be up on your contemporary lit."

"So did your teachers use these books in your classes?"

"I read my own books, Dad. Always have. You *know* this."

I smile again, remembering how she always gravitated toward the children's books with black girls on the cover. I bought her every one of them, as they were in fairly short supply back then.

I fan through the books. I don't readily recognize the names, which further underscores how on-point Jazz is in giving them to me. I feel like I should know these writer's names but haven't gotten quite that far yet. Carlene Brice. Dana Johnson. Roxane Gay. Tayari Jones. Martha Southgate. As I see their names, I remember that I could possibly be teaching this fall, and if I do, maybe I could work some of these into my courses.

"Thank you, baby," I say, hugging her. "I'll start reading these on the flight back to New York."

"Let me know what you think. I'm really curious to hear your thoughts."

"Sure. No problem," I say, hugging her again.

Julio Iglesias had this song "To All the Girls I've Loved Before." It was a hit, too. Not so embedded within the lyrics was the fact that he had unabashedly loved many women. I can relate to that song. Still, if I had to think about the one woman I allowed to get away, hands down it would have been Carmen. I know I will always love her; it's just that I love her enough to leave her alone to have the kind of life she wants for herself and Jazz.

Part of my way of giving her space to do her thing is that I don't unnecessarily linger around the house when I visit. In fact, after I got the books from Jazz, I had planned to ease on back to the hotel for a bit before I checked to see if Jazz might want to grab dinner later. But listening to her talk about her desire to get out of Nashville after graduation and go to Ellison-Wright for college made me a big ball of putty. When I went to college there, it never occurred to me that I would one day have a daughter who would make my alma mater her top choice.

"Jasmine!"

It's Carmen calling from downstairs. I can only imagine what she's thinking after seeing a strange car in the driveway.

"I'm up here with Daddy!"

Jazz opens the door and starts walking toward the stairs. I follow closely behind.

When we make it to the stairs, Carmen is already in the middle of the staircase. She sees me and smiles broadly, and I'm immediately floored by how beautiful she is. She looks like the queen version of her younger self. I've always felt like letting her get away was my biggest mistake, but now I feel the full weight of time on that mistake.

"Hi Marz," she says casually when she reaches the top of the stairs. For a moment Carmen and I look at each other, not really sure of how we should greet each other—even though we have seen each other at least once a year or more since she and Jazz moved here.

I lean in to hug her and she readily accepts my embrace, pressing herself fully against me. The exchange is so brief it goes virtually unnoticed by Jazz. It's been a while since I have wanted Carmen this badly. The fact that she's an amazing woman, not to mention the mother of my child, makes her intoxicating as hell. But I play it cool. After all, there's no use in pining after someone you could never have. Plus, I don't deserve someone like Carmen. Not with my checkered-ass past. My shit is leopard spotty.

"So how was lunch?" Carmen asks.

"Cool," Jazz responds. "We had a good time. Dad even got recognized by a white dude."

I want to tell Jazz that those white dudes were the ones who actually dropped $16.99 for a CD back in the 90s, while the *brothers* were dubbing that shit from their friends or trying to download a pirated copy. But it's not funny with that little coda, so I leave it be.

"Marz, do you have plans for dinner?" Carmen asks.

"No. I'm just chillin'."

"Well, then you should stay for dinner. We're having a few friends over for a kind of pre-birthday dinner, and I'm sure Jasmine would want you to be here—and I would, too."

"Please, Daddy," Jazz says, tugging my arm.

There's no way I can say no to either of them, and I suspect they know this.

I MET Carmen when I was twenty-three and still young in the pro rap game. Marv and I were opening for A Tribe Called Quest at a summer fest sponsored by one of the local radio stations. She told me later that while she liked our first major joint, "Spaced Out," she and her girls had really come out to see Tribe. And that's all good because I will be a Tribe fan until the day I die. Plus, Marv and I were too new to have a big following anyway.

Apparently, her girl scored them some backstage passes. That's when she recognized me from my performance. She sweated me not even the tiniest bit. We could have been standing next to each other in line at a grocery store.

When Q-Tip, Phife, and Ali rolled through, she politely excused herself to go take pictures with them. *Oh well*, I thought, watching her walk away, her voluptuous body packed into a baby-tee and skin tight jeans. I knew I wouldn't see her again once she got around the headliners, but she surprised me and came back a few minutes later to finish up our conversation.

She told me her favorite writer was Octavia Butler and that the futuristic shit Marv and I did was like a take on that. "I like to know black people will be dope in the future," she said.

When her girls scooped her up, she gave me her number and told me to hit her up sometime. It wasn't even on some "I want you" tip. It all started straight-up platonic. And because we weren't coming at each other like that, I kept on my grind with other women. I didn't put it in her face—mainly because I knew she was dope and I wanted to leave my options with her open—but I did my dirt as only a motherfucker like me could.

After six months of hanging out, she put out some feelers to see where my head was. She flirted a lot more, telling me that I couldn't handle all she had to offer and that I couldn't even daydream about the goodies until I had already cleaned my plate. And clean my plate I did—like I was gobbling the last of my Brussels sprouts to get to the chocolate cake. I had never wanted a woman as badly as I wanted Carmen—and that holds true to this day.

I loved her and she loved me back.

And we had a kid.

And I fucked around.

And I apologized.

And I fucked around again.

And she left—with Jazz.

And I have regretted it ever since.

She has since forgiven me, and I have forgiven myself—but neither of us has forgotten the pain I caused. I could never bring myself to hurt her again. Keeping a little distance has made staying out of her life easier, but I realize moving to Nashville will really test my ability to stay in my lane. But if it helps Jazz, I will do what I have to do.

Laird has a modest shop in a gentrified neighborhood. I can tell his days of making jewelry for rappers is over and that his main business is selling engagement rings to twenty-somethings who have six figure salaries.

He greets me with a dap and a hug and eyes me like he hasn't seen anyone from his former life in decades and has missed every minute of it.

"I got you set up over here," he says, walking over to a small table set up in the back of the room. "I think she'll love it," he adds.

On the table is a square white jewelry cloth and an 18k white gold thin-roped chain with a charm scripted in b-girl letters that says "Jazz." I look at it, my heart melting. It's dope.

I know a lot of people who would get other types of gifts for their daughters on a Sweet Sixteen, like a house, a diamond ring, a tennis bracelet, a car, or even some fancy trip to Europe. But Jazz already has most of that stuff, compliments of a dude who, ironically, is campaigning hard to be her ex-stepfather with his antics. I'm an MC. I'm an ambassador for hip-hop, and in every way Jazz is her father's daughter. She will understand this gift, but even more, she will appreciate it. It's really the kind of gift only I could get her where it would have any emotional relevance.

"Wow!" I manage, picking it up and checking it out against the light.

"It gets the Marz Banx stamp of approval?" Laird asks, smiling like he just won a bet for a grand on the Super Bowl.

"Mos def, my man. Dope. Straight-up dope."

"Glad you like it. I haven't done a piece like this one in a minute. It felt good going back to my roots."

"That's what's up."

I pay Laird, tip him, and promise to stay in touch.

As I glance at the box in the small bag, I can't wait to give it to Jazz tomorrow at her party.

CHAPTER EIGHT

Derrick is in and out all evening, claiming to be busy with team-related stuff. What this big-headed corn-fed Negro doesn't get is that Carmen has been down this road before. Hell, I took her there myself. Dude ain't fooling no one, and when he dips out for one of his hours-long errands, I ask Carmen how she's doing. I can see the look in her eyes and know she's up against her breaking point. I don't push her, but I let her know if she needs to talk, I'm here for her. I see a mild relief settle across her face.

It feels funny to be on this side of things, and my heart goes out to Carmen. I want to whisper in her ear again how sorry I am for what I did to her, but now is not the time. She's fighting her own battle now, and all I can do is let her know I'm here for her if she ever feels compelled to use my help.

Jazz has several of her girls over and two guys (whom she says are just friends). At a certain point in the evening the kids take over the den and Carmen and I make our way to a large room that functions as a library. I know this room is Carmen's because there is nothing about Derrick that screams that he reads anything other than a playbook.

"Would you like a drink?" Carmen asks, walking over to a mini-bar she has set up in the corner of the room.

"Sure."

"You still a Cognac and Coke guy?"

"You already know this."

She brings over my drink and sighs. It's not aimed at me, as far as I can tell. I ask again, "Are you all right?"

She takes a long swallow of her own drink. "I know I should be happy because it's Jasmine's birthday weekend, but...," her voice trails off. "I'm just getting tired. That's all."

I take her free hand in mine and pull her into a light embrace. "Carmen, you can talk to me. Is it about Derrick?" I decide to put it out there in hopes of making it easier for her to talk about it.

For a moment she says nothing, gripping her cup like a walking cane, imaginary support, as she stares out into the middle of the room. Finally, she opens her mouth to speak. "I'm not a bitter woman, and I don't want to be a bitter woman. But sometimes you get pushed so far, lied to so much, *disrespected* so much that you have little choice but to despise every man walking the earth." She exhales deeply. "I know I shouldn't cast a shadow over every man, but I've done absolutely nothing to deserve the level of bullshit men have dished out on me during my life."

I want to say something profound, even useful—

really anything to assuage her concerns, but I know I'm part of the problem she laments. I squeeze her tighter, hoping to convey a solidarity that my voice might betray.

She looks at me and for the first time in over a decade, a warmth falls across her face, a familiarity. We are kissing each other before my brain has a chance to make sense of any of this.

"Mom! Dad!"

Carmen jerks away from me, her abruptness leaving me with my arms still hanging in the air.

"What are you two doing?" Jazz's voice is less incredulous and more like genuinely surprised.

Carmen looks at Jazz and offers her the most cliché line available. "Jasmine, it's not how it looks."

And Jazz follows the script accordingly. "Well, it looks like you were kissing my dad."

Even though I could have predicted this dialogue, I can only feel the weight of what this exchange means. So much time has passed since Carmen and I were together that nearly all of Jazz's perceptions of me are as her father, not her mother's former lover. I don't know if she sees this as a kind of betrayal or not. Nonetheless, it's crazy awkward.

If this were a TV show, Jazz would run out of the room, clearly distressed, and the show would cut to a commercial break to leave the audience in suspense. But this isn't TV and Jazz hasn't moved an inch since she entered the library. I can hear her friends laughing and talking down the hall. Then they all get quiet.

"Hey, Mr. Smith," they all say, almost in unison.

With Jazz, Carmen, and I realizing Derrick has

just returned, we silently agree to table this discussion for later as we conspire to make the scene look like anything other than what it really is.

Derrick eventually finds the three of us in the library. We are spaced out inconspicuously (as far as I can tell) like a major triad chord on a piano. With him standing in the doorway, I realize we're actually more of a seventh chord now. I can't tell what he's thinking, but his demeanor is warm.

"Marz Banx is in the house!" he says. His phrasing is so awkward and loud that I half-expect him to reach into the back of his waistband and pull out a nine millimeter to unload on me. He extends his hand to dap me, and I extend my own, waiting for his brute strength to crush my knuckles and cause me to wince in pain in front of Carmen and Jazz.

But he only daps me.

Jazz smiles first, and I follow suit.

"How was your flight down?" he asks, not approaching Carmen or Jazz to say hello.

"Almost missed my flight but I pulled off a Usain Bolt in the airport."

"You mean an O.J. Simpson."

Before my mind pulls up the old 1970s Hertz commercial of O.J. hurdling little kids in the airport, I think about the double murder trial, and it feels as though all of the air has been sucked out the room. When his comment finally resonates, I chuckle slightly and say, "Yeah. O.J."

This is the second time in two days where a dude has walked in on me doing my thing. I am relieved that Carmen and I hadn't escalated to where Noni and I had been.

"Well, I need to put some things away. I'll get up with you guys in a bit." He steps over and kisses Carmen on the forehead and touches Jazz on the shoulder.

"Okay, honey," Carmen says.

Seconds later, Jazz, Carmen, and I are alone again in the library.

"I think I'll leave. I should probably get some sleep. It's been a long day, you know?"

They both nod.

I kiss each of them on the cheek, hop in my rental, and head back to the hotel.

AN HOUR LATER, I get a text message from Jazz.

You still love her, don't you?

I look at the screen of my smart phone. How do I even begin to explain my thoughts to her? She's definitely mature for her age, but this kind of grown folks business is best understood by those who have some life experience.

Your mom will always be special to me. She gave me you, I text.

A few seconds later, Jazz responds, *Well I guess it's a good thing you don't live in Nashville—because if you did, things would get pretty crazy, huh?*

I don't know how to respond. My heart falls like a stone into my stomach. I want to tell her about Vandenheuval University, but the time couldn't be any worse. I'm starting to feel like she wants to keep Carmen and me apart from each other, geographically. I can't possibly have this conversation with her now.

Instead, I type, *LOL!*, and I tell her we can get together for a birthday breakfast, if she's up for it.

She agrees.

CHAPTER NINE

The restaurant Jazz selects for breakfast was featured on a show on the Food Network. It's known for pancakes and homemade syrups, jams, and sauces they make in-house. Jazz admits she's been laying off this kind of food for the past two months so she could look her best for her birthday. "Well, today is my birthday, so I would like to start the day eating something I really want to eat."

I nod. "Enjoy it, baby," I say, ordering the same thing she does.

"Okay, hear me out," she says.

"What's up?"

"I know I haven't talked to Mom yet—but I wanted to run this by you first."

Oh lord, I think. I hope this girl doesn't put me between a rock and a hard place with Carmen. "What is it?"

"Promise me you'll keep an open mind."

"I can do that."

"Okay. I want to move to New York with you and finish out high school there."

"What? You'd give up all of your friends and your school and Carmen and Derrick to come to Harlem?" I don't even mention how logistically challenging that would be, given that I don't know the first thing about the school systems in New York.

"I need to start getting ready for college. I'll keep up with my friends the way I'd do it then. Social media. No biggie. Plus, I think a change would be good."

I have to be careful with my words because I don't want to seem like I'm pushing her away. I know a truth she doesn't, though. New York is not all Rockefeller Plaza and Central Park. There're some harsh realities to living full-time in a city like that. I wouldn't be able to focus on anything if I knew she'd have to take the train everywhere and deal with some of the loud-mouthed kids who bully their way through the city like they're eager to get to Rikers. I think about my neighborhood and how my daughter's fresh face might make her a target for jealous girls who carry razor blades under their tongues and ignorant-ass boys looking for a place to shoot their thug love. Hell to the fucking naw.

And then I think about how I can barely afford to live in New York my damn self. I couldn't afford to raise a teenager there on what I make.

But how do you tell your daughter that she can't move to New York to be with you—and do this on her birthday?

That's when I realize the only way I can turn this situation around is if I tell her everything about Vandenheuval University—now.

And that's what I do.

Jazz's eyes widen as I tell her about the interview,

how I'm planning to move to Nashville to be closer to her, come what may, and how I want to be there for her in a way that I've been unable to do MCing and DJing in New York. For a moment she says nothing, and although I've known her all her life, I swear I can't read her expression.

"You're moving *here*?" she finally says.

"Yes—if I get this job. Well, even if I don't, I want to find something so I can be closer to you."

"Wow," she says, still stunned.

"You wanted to be closer to me, right? So this is an ideal situation."

She nods slowly.

"What's wrong?" I ask. "Seriously. Help me out here."

"It's not that I don't love the idea of us being closer to each other. I was just hoping to get away from Nashville."

"Why? You have a good life here."

"I guess so."

For a minute we sit there in silence. I try to give her time to share a bit more, but I realize this is a serious assumption on my part.

"Are you looking forward to your party?" I ask, awkwardly changing the subject. "I hear DJ Optimus Rhyme is pretty dope."

Jazz's face brightens. "He really is, Daddy. I saw him one time when Badu had to cancel a show I was gonna check out with some friends."

"You're already catching shows? You're able to get into a club at your age?" I know I sound like the most naïve father ever, but what am I supposed to do?

She shrugs like this is no big deal. "I have a friend who works there."

"How old is this friend?"

"She's eighteen, but it's not a bad club. She's a waitress there."

I sigh heavily. "Does this club sell alcohol?"

I know I sound like a father with an ugly Gordon Gartrell sweater when I say this, but I don't want my daughter to turn into some kind of chickenhead that hangs out backstage trying to get on with some dude wearing a platinum chain he hasn't even paid off yet.

"But I don't drink," she says.

It's not an answer to my question, but I decide not to press the issue—at least now, not on her Sweet Sixteen.

I call over the server for the ticket.

"I should probably get you back home so you can get ready for the party."

"Dad, can I tell you something—but you can't tell Mom, okay?"

"Sure."

I lean in closer so she can lower her volume if she wants.

"I think Mom is gonna leave Derrick."

This is hardly surprising after last night's revelation, but I nod my head patiently as I try to feel out where Jazz's head is on all of this.

"He's not even trying to be smooth with his side chicks. I think she's already seen a lawyer because she asked me to help do a search for one on the Internet. We've even talked about what would happen if we ever left Nashville—just me and her."

"That's a lot to think about," I say, taking her hand. "Where did she want to go?"

"That's it! She wants to move to Mississippi! Dad, I can't live in Mississippi. I don't want to be a slave!" she says dramatically.

"Well, I'd hate to know what you think of me, since I'm from Alabama," I respond, laughing. "So that's why you want to move to New York then?"

"Pretty much."

"Well—shit."

"You said it, Dad."

I consider all that she's saying, but my mind is flooded with too many thoughts. "Let's get you home for your party," I say again.

She nods and I leave an extra ten on the table for the server as we bounce.

CHAPTER TEN

When I first started writing rhymes with The Space Modulators, a lot of hip-hop heads accused me of being too cerebral.

"I know some niggas who deep, but you *too* fuckin' deep for most niggas," my boy Swole Nutz used to say. Of course he wasn't really an MC. He was a guy who basically chanted over 808 loops for ringtones. Still, he had a point.

> With a flow so automatic/
> Beyond geographic/
> I spit meters and measures so
>   grammatic/
> Teeth so wise they impacted/
> Heads like "Sirius B?" Seriously?/
> But they don't know where my
>   head be/
> Don't need a chicken hawkin' my
>   Stephen Hawking/
> Only brain from a brain if she talkin'

Dudes used to tell me they'd have to write my

lyrics down and debate their meaning. Nowadays, though, some white teenagers will put my shit up on Rap Genius with their interpretations of my lyrics—which, for the most part, are fairly accurate.

Some days I feel like going back in the studio to work on a new project, but I don't know if the fire is even there any more. I've worked with a lot of producers, a lot of them up and coming, but it's nothing like the chemistry Marv and I had. Maybe teaching is the next level for a Word Jedi like myself. I don't really know. Maybe academics look at rappers like me teaching and feel a way about it—like how some classically trained actors feel when they lose out to some second-rate R&B singer-turned-actor. I'd like to think my masters degree makes me different in that scenario, but I'd be naïve to think some professors see me as anything other than a nigga gripping my nuts with one hand and holding up my pants with the other, stereotypes I've *never* caved in to.

I guess turning forty-years-old really is a crossroads of sorts. About the only think I know is that I want to be a good father. The other shit is hazy. With hip-hop, I have to be honest. My best days are behind me. Still, I can't help feeling that she's not done with me yet, hip-hop that is. Maybe she'll never be done with me—and if that's the case, I'd be cool, 'cause while I can drop the mic, I'll never stop loving H.E.R.

SITTING on the edge of my hotel bed, admiring Laird's handiwork, I wonder what I should tell Jazz.

My fingers trace the outline of her name, and I begin to wonder if I *could* actually take care of Jazz by myself. Hell, she's sixteen. It's not like I'm back to changing diapers. She's mature enough to not be constantly supervised. I could probably squeeze out enough space for her to be okay with sleeping at my place; she just needs a little privacy, so I can take the couch and give her my bed.

Maybe I could pull it off, but maybe, just maybe, my daughter is just overreacting to the uncertainty of all of this stuff. Maybe I could get my own place in Nashville's metro area; that way if Carmen decides to really move to Mississippi, Jazz could stay behind with me. I'm sure life in Nashville would be better for her than anything New York has to offer.

If she had grown up in New York or was planning to go to college there, that would be one thing. But Jazz left before she could really be a city girl, and she's spent most of her life south of the Mason-Dixon. Not to sell my girl short, but I'm a little skeptical of how savvy she would be in Harlem. I know the city is not bad overall, but I don't want her to accidentally wind up being easy pickings for somebody looking to rob a newby.

When I got Carmen to come to New York with me back in the day, I remember that first week some crackhead stole her purse right off her shoulder and was nearly three blocks away when I got out the gate. Never found the motherfucker either. I felt crushed, too. The only reason Carmen was even in the city was because of me, and then she got robbed and I couldn't do anything about it other than run ten blocks before realizing I should have stayed back to protect my girl rather than run deeper into the hood looking for a crackhead I probably wasn't going to find anyway.

I'll be damned if I allow the same thing to happen to Jazz. I would lose my fucking mind if that happened.

So I refuse to let it.

My Plan A, B, and C are all built around moving here and giving her the option to stay with me if she wants.

It's the best I can do for now. I just have to do a better job of selling her on it.

I ROLL up to the house roughly an hour before the party is to start. I figure I can help out a little with setting up things. I'm not early enough to be in the way and not late enough to be useless.

I'm greeted by Derrick in the driveway, his big shit-eating, philandering-ass grin betraying his cordiality. (I should know. I have rocked that same grin.)

"Marz, my man!" he says, dapping me and pulling me into a semi-hug. Being this close to him underscores just how big he really is. I feel like a child and fear for the dudes who have to face off against this fool on football Sundays.

"How's it looking up in there? Y'all need two more hands?"

"Naw, dawg. We got it on lock. You a guest. Just kick back and chill."

I nod.

"But yo, I gotta show you something. You're gonna fuckin' love this!"

I follow him to his man cave in the basement of the house. It's huge and looks like it might run the length of the entire first floor. In the corner of the room is a huge speaker set and a turntable off to the side.

"You a vinyl man, too, right?"

I nod. "Always."

I'm trippin' out that the husband of my baby's mama is trying to impress me with his toys. I think briefly back to Noni's crazy-ass ex, and it takes everything in me to keep from laughing out loud.

Then I hear the opening bass thumps to my song "Do Dat." Marv's production has never sounded so good. I feel like I'm back in the studio with the bass and the kicks, the reverb of the snares echoing, all that classic hip-hop boom-bap thumping in my chest like thunder. My eyes glass up from the intensity of it all.

"Can you feel that shit in your fucking soul?" Derrick says.

It takes everything in me to speak. I finally say, "Damn."

"I know, right?"

I collapse into a nearby recliner and let the music wash over me in thick, heavy waves. The irony of all of this is that I'm the artist, and I can't even afford to hear my own music the way a fan could in the privacy of his own home.

"Marz, I would offer you some bud to kick back to, but I know it's not right to be lit up before Jazz's party."

I laugh, not because he said anything humorous,

but because he's trying to act like he has any values when it comes to my family—and in my mind that includes Carmen, too. Under any other circumstances, he and I could have probably been cool, but that ain't the case here and now.

"I should probably let Jazz know I'm here so I can see if she needs anything," I say.

"Bet. I need to make sure Kung-Fu Joe is setting up his shit in the right spot."

"Kung-Fu Joe?"

"Yeah. That DJ Jazz wanted."

"Optimus Rhyme," I say, ignoring his attempt at racist humor.

"Yeah, that dude."

I find Carmen whisking through the hall, headed for the the kitchen. She stops when she sees me.

Cliché: "About last night..."

"I know," I respond. "Dope, wasn't it?"

She rests her hand on my chest and opens her mouth to say something. Instead she smiles to herself, pushes me away, and walks off. "Jazz is out back," she calls to me over her shoulder.

I really want to talk to her, to apologize for all the pain I've ever caused her, to tell her that I've never stopped loving her, to let her know I'd be different this time around, if she ever wanted to come back to me, but I don't. Maybe this fantasy I have of her is all I will ever have, so I have to be cool with that. Plus, it's not about me anymore; it's about Jazz.

I find Jazz out back talking to one of her friends.

When she sees me, she beckons me over to say hello to her friend LaTasha, the one who does the open mics, she reminds me. Jazz is in a really good mood, and it warms my heart to see her looking much less stressed than she had been at breakfast.

"Do you need help with anything?" I ask her.

"I'm good, Dad. Thanks."

"Well, I'm going to float around and try to make myself useful."

"Okay," Jazz responds, smiling.

As I walk away, I can hear Jazz's friend saying, "Do you think he would be okay if I ask for a picture with him?"

"Girl, my dad is real cool about stuff like that."

I turn around and head back to take the picture, before adding, "Keep doing your poetry. I like that my daughter has friends who are creatives."

Jazz is a good sport about this fan moment, and when I kiss her on the cheek before walking away, she pushes me away in the same playful way that Carmen did only moments earlier.

Optimus Rhyme is setting up his equipment when I walk over and dap him up.

"Thanks for doing this for my daughter," I say.

"Marz Banx?" he says, actually looking at me more closely. "Wow! They didn't tell me that you'd be here. I'm a fan, for real," he says.

"I appreciate it. I'm looking forward to hearing your set."

"For sure. Any special requests?"

"Yeah," I respond. "Anything Jazz wants to hear."

He laughs. "Sure thing."

I want so badly to ease my way back into the kitchen to sidle up next to Carmen, but I know that's not the smartest thing to do with all of these people around. Plus, I know Jazz is watching me around her mother, and I have no clue what to think about Derrick emerging out of thin air, like a mountain cutting through the fog.

As I consider what to do with myself next, I busy myself by checking my email from my smart phone. There's a message from Vandenheuval University at the top of my unread list. It's not from the dean; it's from Dr. Delaney. It's surprisingly short, but the gist of the email is that they've decided to go in a different direction and that they will not be extending an offer to me.

I put my phone back in my pocket, surprised at how defeated I feel. What the hell happened? It was supposed to be a sure thing. I gave that interview everything I had. Maybe I was just kidding myself into thinking I could be a professor, that I could be anything other than a washed up MC.

I have failed my daughter again.

I look around at all of the fancy decorations, the DJ, the people, all of it, and I let it settle over me that I didn't pay for any of this shit. I'm a fucking guest. Another man is footing the bill for my family because of my life choices. I'm not the crying type, but I feel the pain so deeply in my gut that I wish I could just disappear for a while until I felt like a man again.

CHAPTER ELEVEN

Jazz's birthday party has a pretty loose structure, with people milling about while Optimus Rhyme does his thing. As I move around and mingle with the guests, I'm still stewing over the email from Dr. Delaney. Deep down, I don't blame him, but because he was an ass during the earlier part of the interview process, he's a convenient object of my ire. The reason I didn't get the job is because I'm not a teacher; I'm an MC.

On Monday, I'll hit up Caldwell and get him to make some moves for me. Maybe I could still cobble together enough to get an apartment for a year or two down here. After that, Jazz will be off to college. Surely I could afford to live down here till then. Hell, every place is cheaper than New York City.

These thoughts help settle me down a bit. I can still make this thing work. I definitely have the inspiration to pull it all together: Jazz.

Optimus Rhyme lowers the music and everyone turns to see Carmen and Derrick pushing in this gigantic Sweet Sixteen cake. Carmen beckons for me to join them. Jazz approaches, and together we form a semi-circle in front of her friends and guests. Optimus brings a microphone over to Carmen, and she taps on it before speaking.

"First, we'd like to thank everyone for coming out to celebrate our baby girl's Sweet Sixteen." The crowd cheers, and she continues, "Jazz, we just want to let you know how proud of you we are and how much we love you."

Jazz embraces Carmen, then me, then Derrick. We're just one big happy family, I muse.

Carmen lights the candles on the cake and we sing "Happy Birthday." Afterwards, Jazz blows out the candles with the kind of lungs only her dad could have given her.

"So for your sixteenth birthday, we wanted to do something special for you," Carmen says, handing Jazz a small box, roughly the same size as the box I have tucked away in my pocket.

"What's this?" Jazz says.

"Just open it," Carmen responds.

Jazz unwraps the box and quickly opens it. We all stare, already knowing what's inside.

Cue cliché: Jazz pulls Mercedes keys from the box and the party erupts in cheers.

Jazz darts through the crowd of people around to the front of the house, where she finds this brand new baby Benz in the driveway, bow on it and all. Smart phone cameras are flashing and Jazz is jumping up and down hugging Carmen, and then Derrick. I am standing nearby, and while she knows I had absolutely nothing to do with this gift, she hugs me, too.

"Wow!" she repeats, almost exhausted from the excitement. "Thank you so much!"

She sits in the driver's seat and places her hands on the steering wheel, and in that moment I realize just how much my baby girl has grown up.

Then I have a second feeling that dulls the first one: Derrick and Carmen, even though they are damn near estranged, have come together to give her a gift I could have never afforded, even when my shit was hot in the streets. I can feel the box I picked up from Laird in my pocket, and now I'm wondering if I should even take it out and give it to her in front of these people. I'll just give it to her later.

Eventually we all return to the backyard where Optimus continues spinning (or pushing the play button or whatever it is he does). I continue to stand around, a shit-eating grin on my face, wanting to be there for my daughter, but feeling more like an inadequate prop to her current lifestyle.

As I stand there looking around, I feel some arms wrapping around my waist from behind.

"Daddy," Jazz says. "I love you."

"I love you, too." I don't know where this is coming from, but a father never gets tired of hearing those words from his daughter.

Then she leans closer to my ear. "I still want to leave here."

I nod. "Yeah. I'm sure you do."

She walks around and holds my arm. "Don't get me wrong. A Benz is crazy! But I still want to come live with you."

"I didn't get the job," I blurt out. I have no idea of why I'm telling her this. Kids shouldn't have to carry the weight of grown folks' problems.

"It's okay. You'll get something else, something better."

I smile, and like that, I have no fucks left to give about the Vandenheuval situation. If my baby girl is good, I'm good.

"So what did you get me?" she asks playfully.

"How do you know I didn't chip in on the Benz?"

"You don't do those kinds of gifts. That's not what you're about. That's the kind of gift that Derrick and Mom would get because they saw someone on TV getting one."

"Still, it's a pretty sweet whip."

"No doubt," she responds. "But what did *you* get me?"

"I'll give it to you later—after the party."

"Daddy," she pleads.

I want to be stiff on this point, if for no other reason than to draw out suspense—or better yet, let my embarrassment from earlier subside.

I reach in my pocket and pull out the box.

"You got me a car, too?" she says, laughing.

"Laugh it up, Jazz," I say.

Before I can think of a more creative comeback, she is holding open the box with tears in her eyes. In that moment I don't know if she's happy or disappointed.

"You got me a chain," she says—and I still can't read her tone.

"Yeah," I utter. "I had the guy who used to do my chains back in the day to hook you up with your own."

She stares at the chain for a moment and then throws her arms around me. "I love it so much!"

I sigh deeply, as she squeezes me tighter.

She takes the chain out of the box and asks if I

would put it around her neck. Once I close the clasp, she faces me and does a b-girl pose. "How do I look?"

It takes everything in me not to lose my shit right there. Back before she was born, I wondered if my child would be able to appreciate hip-hop as a culture, if my child would see me as a contributor to the art form. As an MC, I really just wanted my child to "get" what it is that I have devoted my life to.

"You look dope," I finally respond.

"Well, you know that you have to rock the mic for my party now that you've got me a rope," she says.

"Are you serious?"

"Mos def, Dad. I want you to do a song for my party."

She tugs me toward Optimus's setup. "My dad is gonna spit some bars," she tells him, and he smiles, handing me the mic.

Jazz grabs the mic from me and says loudly, for everyone to hear, "Excuse me, everyone! Excuse me! My father, the legendary Marz Banx, is gonna perform!"

At this, the crowd, in this strange fluid motion, moves toward the DJ area where we're standing. I can see Carmen in the back, smiling, and across from her on the other side of the crowd, I see Derrick pumping his hands, geeked out. I smile when I consider that both my ex-girl and her man are fans, but they can barely stand each other now.

I look at Jazz. "So what do you want to hear?"

"I don't know. Surprise me."

Shortly after Jazz was born, Marv and I cut a track about what it felt like to be a new father, and what it meant for me, a notorious ladies man, to confront the karma of my own actions in the form of my daughter. How could I shield her from knuckleheads like me? The song resolves itself by my talking about the fact that I have to be a better example for her. The song was tentatively called "Baby Girl," but the label didn't think we should include it on the LP because it was so outside of what we were going for with the concept project. We never could find an LP to put it on, so we never released it. While I have a number of songs no one has ever heard before, this is by far the most apropos of any of them.

I scan through my memory bank and tell Optimus to drop an instrumental at 88 beats per minute. For the next six minutes I perform a song that I thought I would never share with the public. As I look at Jazz, I remember seeing her emerge from her mother sixteen years ago, her tiny body stretching, trying to reconcile itself to this new space. I see her being weighed and measured. I see her in that isolette, with the lamps blasting on her to cure her jaundice. I see her smiling in her sleep. I see her getting bigger and doing new things. I am remembering every milestone. And then I relive Carmen taking her to Nashville, and I relive the pain. But through the years, she has continued to grow and get more beautiful and smarter and more talented. She became my raison d'être. And the words of this song are stretching themselves to be all of these emotions that I feel in this moment.

When I finish, I see only Jazz, her tear-filled eyes looking up at me, and I realize that, while I don't have a lot of resources in this life, my daughter appreciates those that I do have.

BY THE TIME the party ends, I am just as exhausted as Carmen. Derrick has said that he had to head out for a business meeting going down in a few, and rather than argue with him over his transgressions, Carmen sighs and waves him off. I can tell in that short moment that whatever she and Derrick had is now dead. He just hasn't realized it yet.

By 9 p.m., the only people left at the house are Carmen, Jazz, and me—and Jazz looks like she is about to pass out. Who could blame her, though, with all the highs and lows of the day and all of that entertaining of people? I would have been worn down to a nub a long time ago.

"Dad," she says, dragging herself along slowly toward the staircase. "When does your plane head out?"

"Tomorrow afternoon. I'll be around in the morning, if you wanna get breakfast before I leave."

"Cool. Let's do that," she responds. "Plus, I still want to talk to you about that thing we were discussing."

I nod my head. "Sure. No problem."

She walks over to me and gives me a tired hug and heads upstairs to her room.

"So what's this thing you and Jasmine are discussing?" Carmen asks, as she walks past me, toward the kitchen.

I follow.

"You know. Just father/daughter stuff."

"Okay," she says, eyeing me suspiciously. "But if it has anything to do with me, please don't leave me twisting in the wind."

"Nah. It's not like that."

I can't tell if I'm lying or not. I probably am—but to admit any more than that is to get all up in the mix between Carmen and Derrick, something that I'm not prepared to do at this point.

Carmen begins putting away things, so I ask if I can help.

"If you could take these garbage bags out back, that would be cool. Derrick should've taken them out before he left, but, well, you know, it's not even worth the drama. He's been missing in action for a minute now."

I grab the bags and say, "No problem. I got it."

As I walk through the back door around to the trash bins, I still can't get over how much space they have at this house. Things must be really jacked up if Jazz wants to shoot the deuces to this kind of opulence and come and crash at my cubbyhole for two years straight.

I walk back to the kitchen. I imagine that Jazz is either in her bed about to pass out or grabbing a bubble bath, which she tends to like after long days. Carmen has taken a seat at on one of the barstools around the island off to the side of the kitchen.

"How're you holding up?" I say, taking a seat next to her.

"All and all, it was a good day. Jazz looked pretty happy about everything."

"A Benz? I would definitely agree."

"It was the least we could do."

I nod, not really understanding what she means but not wanting to push.

"For all of the shit Derrick has put me through, the least he could do was get my baby a Benz."

I don't have a response. I can't really argue if the beneficiary of this power play is my daughter. I don't know what Derrick owes Carmen, but I imagine that this Benz is scratching the surface of what she's going to take in the divorce. I don't have to use that word—divorce—though. It's all in the air like the smell of chitterlings.

"About last night," she starts. "We should probably clear the air."

"There's no need to say anything."

"Yes, there is. We both know that nothing can ever happen with us, so there's no point in complicating things, especially when everything has been working so well."

"I see."

"You have different thoughts? Talk to me, Marz. What's on your mind? You've never been that good at hiding your feelings."

"I'm good."

She sucks her teeth. "I need for you to be straight up with me. My life is all over the place right now, so I need you to be one of those things that I can count on."

I consider playing her off to the side, but I know I won't do that. Not to Carmen.

"I didn't see last night as a mistake."

She doesn't respond, so I continue.

"I have never really tried to hide my feelings for you when you get right down to it. I just always stepped back and gave you space. I owed you that, especially after all of the stupid shit I put you through."

I am looking directly into her eyes, but I can't read them anymore than I could Jazz's earlier.

I soldier on. "Last night reminded me of how much I have missed having you this close to me. It felt like back in the day—the three of us, you know?"

Carmen shifts in her seat as she considers this. "Marz, I'm not going to say that I don't still have some feelings for you buried deep inside of me—I guess last night they just bubbled up to the surface—but you put me through a lot, too. You really hurt me."

I lower my head, feeling the weight of my past transgressions. "I know. I'm really sorry. I know you deserve more than all of this."

She sighs. "I'm not blaming you for what Derrick has done. I'm just trying to be smart about my life going forward. Do you realize that I have not been without a relationship for nearly twenty years? And the two men I gave my love to cheated on me. That's a hard pill to swallow. I just want Jasmine and me to enjoy these last two years before she goes to college without all of the in-house drama."

"She asked to come and live with me." I don't know why I say this, but it just jumps off my lips without any thought.

"She wants to live with *you?*" As Carmen says this, there is a sobering look dawning on her face, as if she has never considered the real possibility Jazz would want to be with anyone other than her. "But," she starts, but she is dumbfounded into silence.

"She doesn't want to move to Alabama. She wants to come to New York," I say. "But I was trying to move down here to be closer. That job fell through, though."

Carmen shakes her head, still in disbelief. "I'm confused. What are you talking about?"

So I walk her through everything that I have been trying to do and why I've been trying to do it, and in the midst of this revelation, I realize just how much I should have consulted her before I had done any of it. But there it is, regardless, laid bare for her to see.

"Wow," she finally says, before standing up. She walks over to the refrigerator and takes out a wine cooler. This time she doesn't sit down; instead, she stands across from me.

"I don't even know what to say." She pauses. "My daughter is planning her life based on my marriage. And her father is conspiring with her."

"It's not like that, Carmen. You know it. She's just worried. And me, I just want to see my baby girl more. No one is trying to hurt you."

"That's it," she says. "It doesn't matter what your intentions are. The result is the same."

"Baby," I say, reaching for her hand. I expect her to move it, but she doesn't. "Maybe one day we can be a family again," I say, as I walk around to her.

We kiss for a moment, and she pushes me back. "I think you need to leave. This is too much for me. I'm going through a lot right now."

I lean in to kiss her again, but her hand presses against my chest, stopping me, just shy of her lips.

"I'll leave, but I want you to know that I still love you, and if you ever give me another chance, I would be the man that you deserve."

She doesn't respond. Instead, she tells me that I should probably go before Derrick returns and gets suspicious.

"Tell Jazz to call me when she gets up. I want to grab breakfast with her before I catch my flight."

Carmen nods her head. "I'll tell her."

I walk toward the door and then turn back. I want to say more, but I don't. I just nod at her and walk back to my car.

CHAPTER TWELVE

Jazz meets me at the IHOP near my hotel. She's in her new car, and a part of me smiles when I see her emerge from it, looking like a million bucks.

"I see you!" I say as she walks over to the table I have already gotten for us. I stand up and give her a big hug. "How are you feeling this morning?"

"I'm good. Just tired," she says, sliding into the seat on the opposite side of the booth.

"Your mom and I had a talk last night."

"Yeah, she told me."

The server comes to the table and takes our orders before we continue.

"We should probably include her in whatever plans we have," I say. "That would only be fair."

Jazz lowers her face. "Yeah, I know."

"I don't know what's gonna happen with your moms and your stepdad—or when it's gonna happen—but know this, I love you more than life itself. This Vandenheuval thing I was telling you about fell through, but I'm still gonna find a way for us to spend more time. I promise you that. Okay?"

"Okay."

"Do you believe me?"

"Yes, Dad."

When the server returns, we eat our breakfast in silence. I want to say more, but I know if I keep talking, I'll just start making stuff up, stuff that I have no way of being able to back up at this point, with no job options down here and a confusing situation with Carmen.

"You want to come up for Thanksgiving this year? I can fry a turkey and see if Ma Dukes can whip up her dressing and potato salad. When's the last time you saw your grandparents?"

"Last year."

"So let's make it happen. We can check with your moms and see if she's cool with that. Maybe, depending on how things are going in her life, she could come with you. I just wanted to extend the invitation."

"Okay," she says, but as I look into Jazz's eyes, I know that she really wants much more than a visit for one of the holidays. Hell, I want more than that, too, but the situation, as it stands, is still unresolved. We have to do what we have to do until we can do what we want to do. There's still time before she heads to Atlanta for college.

When we finish our meal, I walk her out to her car.

"I'm gonna call you as soon as I get back to New York, okay?"

"Okay, Dad," she says, hugging me around my waist.

"We are gonna make this happen. Straight up.

You just keep those grades up so you can get a scholarship to Ellison-Wright, a'ight?"

"I got you."

"I know you do," I respond, hugging her.

I watch her get into her car and keep my eyes on her until her car is no longer in view.

I MAKE it to the airport early so I can avoid the same situation I had when I flew here. In fact, I'm early. Two hours early for a Sunday morning flight. I have nothing to pass the time but the music on my phone and a copy of *Slay 'Em*'s last issue (the latest one with the "greatest MCs" hasn't dropped yet).

My mind is swirling as I replay the entire weekend, from my hook up with Noni to that last conversation with Carmen. The only thing that rumbles with any real gravity is the look on Jazz's face when I rapped for her at her birthday party. I have to remind myself that, no matter what, everything I do going forward needs to be for my baby girl.

My phone wallpaper is Jazz's most recent school picture. People always joke around about the idea of a daddy's girl, but what they don't really think about is how the daddy feels about his daughter. Outside of Carmen, there is no one in the world who could possibly care as much for that girl as I do. No one, outside of Carmen, knows just how far Jazz has come, from that NICU isolette to being the smart, beautiful young lady she is today.

I'm going to find a way to be closer to her. I just have to figure out something that makes sense, now that I'm back to the drawing board.

As I listen to my favorite MC, Phonte, my phone rings with an unfamiliar number. The first thing I wonder is who could possibly be calling this number on a Sunday afternoon, especially with an Atlanta area code. With nothing to lose, I answer.

"Hello?"

"Hello. May I speak to Mr. Banks?"

"This is he."

"Mr. Banks, my name is Raphael Stephens, and I'm the chair of the music department at Harlington College, just outside of Atlanta. I hope you don't mind me calling you like this, but I got your number from my friend Theo Butler at Vandenheuval. He told me that for some reason they couldn't take you on over there, but that you might be still be interested in teaching."

I am floored. A possible job? I had abandoned the idea of trying this again—ever. But there's a part of me that's more than intrigued, a part that never gave up the idea.

And Atlanta? It's much closer to Nashville than New York, and my baby girl will be headed there for college. I'd be close enough to her if she needed me and far enough away if she didn't. I'm actually surprised that Atlanta never crossed my mind.

"Mr. Banks?"

"Yes," I finally say, unable to stop smiling. "I am definitely interested. What did you have in mind?"

-fin-

THE IMPERSONATOR

A Bonus Story

When I was growing up, adults would often ask each other what they were doing when certain major events took place. They were usually referring to the assassinations of President John F. Kennedy and Martin Luther King, Jr. I was baffled how they could recollect with such peculiar accuracy what was going on around them in those moments. When I grew older, the death of the rapper Hannibal Streets would become one of those "what were you doing when" moments for my generation.

I remember very vividly what I was doing when I heard the news of his passing, mainly because I was preparing to do a stand-up routine at Hosea's Amateur Comedy Night, where I had prepared some jokes about Hannibal. I ultimately decided against telling those jokes—which were largely impersonations—and ended up bombing, although the largely grieving audience was merciful. If I had been a halfway decent comedian, I could have flipped my act that night and used those impersonations to comfort and uplift the spirits of my audience. The shock of the news at that moment, though, impaired my judgment, and I panicked.

A year later I ventured into another open-mic amateur night and did the original Hannibal routine. It got a few laughs, but it didn't completely slay the audience, as I had hoped. Afterwards, however, a few people came up to me and complimented me on my impersonation. Unbeknownst to me at the time, one of those people would eventually take my career to the next level.

Hannibal Street's rise to becoming arguably the greatest emcee of all time started inauspiciously with him serving as a roadie and background dancer for a West Coast rap group called Kilobytes. But you probably already know most of this, since his bio has been rehashed thousands of times by every news source covering entertainment the world over. During his seven years in the music business, he released three platinum-selling albums before being murdered outside of the Super Bowl in 1997. But I'm sure you already know that, too.

Probably one of the most fascinating things about Hannibal was how prolific an artist he had been, especially once he completed a two-year stint in prison for the alleged sexual assault of a beauty queen (an issue relentlessly debated by fans well after he had already served his time). His second album (or first since his release) was a double LP that went four times platinum. His third LP sold nearly six million units. After his death, rumors circulated that he had damn near five hundred songs locked away in some vault, heavily guarded by his record label, Three Strikes. As a result, almost like clockwork, Three Strikes drops a new Hannibal Streets LP each year, showcasing some hot new producer the label is looking to promote.

It's all quite a story, really. It's like one of the greatest emcees of all time never really died (don't get me started on the rumors that he faked his death). This is the public narrative as we know it, and it is the story my daughter, Zina, knows.

But it's not the only story there is.

There's also my story.

On the night I was finally able to perform my Hannibal Streets routine, I met a guy name Eli Jones, who introduced himself as the owner of a talent agency of the same name. Roughly 5'5", he was full of confidence and knew just how to approach me to get me to sign on as a client. He gushed over my comedic timing, my choice of material, and my level of comfort in front of an audience. What really floored him, though, was what he referred to as a spot-on impersonation of Hannibal Streets. Up till that point, I had thought my impersonation as just good enough—definitely not spot-on.

"Who you kiddin'?" Eli responded. "I closed my eyes and thought that nigga was still alive."

"Well, you know what some people say," I offered, referring to the conspiracy theorists.

"Whatever, man. What I do know is that you sound just like that motherfucker. Don't look a damn thing like him, but I bet you could fool his mama on the phone."

"Really?" I asked. "Did you know him personally?"

"Yeah, I knew him. That's why I know what the fuck I'm talkin' 'bout."

His interest seemed genuine enough, so I signed with him. I thought he might help me get booked at a few places—maybe set me up for the occasional talk show appearance. That was not his plan for me, he told me. "Let's go make some *real* money."

To me, in my naiveté, that meant an HBO show or something on Netflix, but it wouldn't be long before the I realized who my employer for the next decade would be: Three Strikes Records.

Back when Three Strikes first started, they owned one studio at the back end of a shopping center, and most of the music production was done by one person, Infinite Design. In fact, music journalists are quick to point out that the "sound" of Three Strikes was built on the back of that single producer. Hannibal's rise to success was likely accelerated by Infinite Design's beats, but later on, after Infinite Design left the label, Hannibal Streets's voice became the strongest cachet for Three Strikes. I guess the thinking was that they could cultivate a whole new crop of producers as long as they had Hannibal's voice to anchor the tracks.

Once Eli introduced me to the executive team over at Three Strikes, I came to see things a bit differently.

"Eli tells me great things about you," Gamma, the CEO, said, shaking my hand.

I was floored by the compliment. I had never met a black man who was listed on the Forbes 400 Wealthiest Americans list. He could have told me he shit strawberries, and I would have believed him.

"I hear you do a pretty good Hannibal," he said.

"I try."

"Do you know any of his songs by heart?"

"A few," I responded.

"Well, let me hear you spit something then."

I thought for a moment, fighting my nerves with each passing second. I figured I'd just do the latest song I'd heard of Hannibal's on the radio a few weeks earlier.

As I launched into the rap, Gamma's eyes grew larger. He stopped me halfway through the second verse.

"Gotdamn, Eli!" he said. "I thought you was just fuckin' with me."

"I told you," Eli responded. "Sounds just like that motherfucker, don't it?"

Gamma nodded enthusiastically, tugging on his rugged goatee. "Well, then. Let's talk turkey. You wanna call it consulting? How about 100 grand per project?"

"I was thinking more like 150 and a finder's fee," Eli said.

"Hey, what's going on here?" I finally piped up.

"I'm negotiating your contract," Eli said.

"But what exactly am I being hired to do?"

"He don't know?" Gamma said.

"Well, I wanted to wait and see if you liked him first," Eli responded.

"Can someone please fill me in?" I asked.

Gamma looked at me and smiled. "No problem. Let me break it down for you."

Over the next hour Gamma explained everything to me, as Eli stood by, patiently nodding. Apparently, the infamous vault of recorded material by Hannibal Streets, while once voluminous, had all but dried up, yet his album sales were higher than ever.

"At first it was just a crazy theory, since I've never heard anyone sound enough like Hannibal to pull it off," Gamma said. "Son, what I'm offering you is an opportunity. If you're not interested, we never had this conversation. You feel me?"

"Yes, sir," I said, suddenly realizing what was being asked of me.

"*Sir?*" Gamma responded, looking at Ali, yet pointing at me. "I like this little nigga."

Shortly after that meeting, Eli negotiated a contract with me that, due to the sensitive nature of our dealings, would allow me to be paid six figures in cash per LP. The only problem was that, beyond my imitations of Hannibal, I couldn't actually rap to save my life.

As fate would have it, I didn't have to be a rapper at all—just a voice impersonator. Gamma had already assembled a small production team of up and coming producers and ghostwriters. The ghostwriters would pen the raps and show me the intonations, inflections, and rhythms. In many ways I found their roles far more difficult than my own.

They were the ones perpetually tasked with going into the creative mind of Hannibal Streets and asking themselves what he might have said and how he might have said it. They had to be both rapper and speechwriter. All I had to do was imitate Hannibal's voice, but, according to everyone involved, that apparently was the hardest part of the equation. I was told no one had ever mastered Hannibal's uniquely raspy voice and his energetic and rhythmic cadence.

We did nearly one hundred songs before my girlfriend told me that we were expecting. Few things can make you reassess your life like the awareness that you are about to be a parent. Still, I kept on with Three Strikes.

I found doing Hannibal to be fun, a way of stepping outside of my regular life and becoming someone else. At times, while recording, I would not just imitate Hannibal's voice; I would imitate his mannerisms, bouncing on the balls of my feet as I spoke, throwing my arms back and forth so that my body swayed in his familiar rhythm. I would close my eyes and imagine I *was* really him. The producers ate it up. So did the public, as Hannibal's records continued to sell through the roof.

In retrospect, I sometimes feel that the public had to know of our ruse. I was convinced that maybe we all wanted to believe Hannibal had an inexhaustible supply of unreleased material sitting in a vault somewhere. Or maybe the conspiracy theorists were right: Hannibal had in fact faked his death and was now living his life in seclusion out in Cuba or some island out in the Caribbean.

I knew better, but I allowed myself to get caught up in all of it. Even as I saw my daughter growing up beside me, I felt more than a financial obligation to uphold the legacy of Hannibal Streets. His life's work was now my life's work.

And I thought I would always be fine with that.

Then one day my daughter, who was now twelve, came up to me and asked me a very simple questions that I should have long ago expected (but had never gotten) that put me into a bit of a tailspin: "Dad, what do you do for a living?"

I thought about telling her that I was a voice actor or a consultant for a record label or something like that (all variations of the truth), but I found myself unable to really articulate any of these thoughts for fear that she would ask me follow-up questions I was unprepared to answer. I was a man who couldn't answer a simple question, and sadly, that question gave way to a far more paralyzing question: who had I become?

Twelve hours out of the day I was a father, a guy who rooted for all of the local sports teams, a guy who lived to binge-watch newly discovered TV shows on Netflix. The other twelve hours, though, I was a musical—a spiritual—conduit for one of the greatest emcees to ever live. There was no greater high, except for the day that my daughter was born. During those twelve hours, I would talk like Hannibal, move like him, even try to eat like I imagined he would eat. The producers at Three Strikes gave me the space to inhabit Hannibal however I could, and I did that. I did my best to become him. The albums kept coming, and I never took my foot off the gas. I had come to a point where I had to impersonate the self that I once was so as to not betray those in my life before all of this began.

I had become a nameless ghost that moved from voice to voice, body to body, and no one, not even I, was the wiser. I had lost myself, all while attempting to become someone I could never become.

When I approached Gamma about walking away to start a new life and be a respectable father to my daughter, I had half-expected him to have one of his goons beat me to a pulp in the lobby of Three Strikes. There was definitely a time when he might have done that, if only to maintain his rep as the no-shit taking ex-con mogul of a record company specializing in gangsta rap. But I knew he wouldn't. For one, the work I did for him was too confidential to invite any attention. Second, I had cut him more songs than even Hannibal had, and the company would be good for at least another decade. But the main reason I knew I would be able to walk away in one piece was because I wasn't the only one who had changed over the years. We all had. Gamma was now spending more time with his own kids, as his oldest son was preparing to accept a lacrosse scholarship to Hampton University in the fall.

We parted ways with a half-hug/half-handshake and his insistence that I take another $25,000 for severance.

These days I spend my work hours on the stage at any comedy club that will host me. So Dad is now a struggling comedian, my daughter often says, before adding, "How is that even possible when you're not even funny around the house?"

Maybe not, I think and then smile to myself. It's so hard to know these days what's really funny. Occasionally I want to break out my Hannibal impersonation—go for the lowest hanging fruit—but I resist. That part of my life is now behind me. What lies ahead, though, I am still attempting to figure out.

* *This story originally appeared in* Black Hand Side: Stories *by Ran Walker.*

16 BARS

A Bonus Story

When I revealed to my freshman composition class that I used to rock the mic as an emcee, nearly all of them doubled over laughing and slapping their desks. One kid even went as far as to ask permission to go to the restroom so he didn't piss himself from hysteria. I knew that they might find the idea of Professor Dennis with a high-top skin-fade and a gold rope amusing, but the wind from their laughter actually cut me a little. I continued on with my discussion about whether certain rappers should be included in our current literary canon, but even when I finished class, I could hear the resounding echo of their laughter still ringing in my ears. I wanted more than anything to show them that I had never been and would never be some wack dude in a tweed coat and tighty whiteys, completely out of touch with hip-hop.

As I slid my laptop into my book bag, I saw Noble Williams lingering behind the group exiting the room. He eased up to the desk, monster headphones resting around his thick neck and a slim notebook in his hand—no textbook to be found, and said, "Professor Dennis, you for real about being an emcee?"

"Yes," I responded. "I used to battle back in the day in Memphis."

"Yo, that's what's up. You think you still nice with yours?"

"Mr. Williams," I said, addressing him in the manner in which I had become accustomed to addressing my students, "I can definitely hold my own."

Noble nodded his head. "Well, yo, I got this mixtape I'm tryna throw up on the Internet in a few months. You wanna spit sixteen on a track?"

"Are you serious?" I responded, still trying to process his question. I hadn't rapped in any serious way since college, although I sometimes freestyled for my five-year-old daughter on our weekend drives. But flowing about Dora the Explorer was not what Noble was asking me to do.

"I'm just sayin," Noble started. "I think it'd be a good look to have my prof on a track letting loose. If you really about yours, folks ain't gonna laugh at you. That's my word."

Maybe it was the thought of silencing my students once and for all or maybe it was the desire to be hunkered over a microphone in a studio reliving my dreams from when I was younger, but whatever it was, I told him I would do it.

It wasn't until I got home and told my wife about it that I realized I might've been in over my head.

The ensuing conversation with my wife was comical in its brevity.

"Baby, should I do it?"

"Sure."

My wife had never heard me rap and didn't even know that I used to harbor fantasies of rocking the mic back in the day, years before I majored in English at FAMU and went on to grad school.

"What if I suck?" I asked.

"Then you'll just suck, and we'll move on."

If it weren't for her staring directly at me, holding one of my hands in hers as she said these things, I might have thought she was being dismissive of the whole thing. Even my daughter, Lena, smiled and clapped her hands when I told her that her daddy was going to be on a rap song.

Now I was definitely locked in, but I hadn't done my thing in so long I wondered if I could even do it anymore. That night I downloaded some instrumental tracks from some of my favorite rappers of the last three years, and sat down with one of my tablets trying to get some inspiration. What could I talk about? I was a husband, a father, and a teacher. I didn't think any of that would be what Noble was looking for, although I knew a lot of rappers were married with children. Back when I was rapping, we either rapped about our DJs or ourselves, pretty much the usual bragging about our own hotness or what neighborhoods we represented.

I knew up front I couldn't do anything hard edged because that wasn't me, so I scanned through music by the PhD kids, rappers whose mothers had doctorates, to see what they were talking about. So there I was, earbuds in my ears playing Mos, Talib, Common, and Kanye nonstop for the next three hours. The more I listened, the more I realized that it was much easier for me to analyze their lyrics than it was for me to write my own.

Two days later when my composition class ended for the day, Noble came back to me, a broad grin on his usually solemn face.

"You good, prof?" he asked.

"Yeah. How is everything with you?"

"Just trying to get this track together. You free this weekend? My boys and I got the studio on lock for a few hours and we wanna get some tracks laid."

The immediacy of it all caught me off guard, and I felt like I had just awakened to find myself standing on the ledge of a building. "Yes, I think I can get away for a few hours," I said, trying to ignore the numbness swarming over my legs.

"A'ight. We doin' this track about hoodin' and nerdin'."

"Like Lupe's 'I'm Beaming?'" I said.

Noble nodded his head. "That's what's up, prof. You know what I'm talkin' about. So just come prepared to spit sixteen bars on that."

I nodded, as if I did sixteen bars every day of my life and it was no big thing. Noble took a sheet of paper out of his bag and scribbled an address and cell phone number on it. "Come through around five, and we'll try to get you done first."

"Cool," I said.

He dapped me and walked out of the classroom. I had to admire his focus. He didn't say much in class, but he kept an "A" average. In fact, his work was among the best in the class, so I figured if he brought that same focus to his music, then he would set a pretty high bar for the song.

As I walked out of the room, I realized that there was a strong probability that I would be the weakest emcee on the track, and I couldn't go out like that. My father used to tell me whenever I went out of town on trips back in high school, "Don't do anything to embarrass yourself, your family, or the Black race." So I understood very clearly that whatever I did, I would have to at least represent on a level as to not embarrass Noble, myself, my wife and daughter, or my father. Oh yeah, and the Black race.

The very first time I battled another emcee was when I was in the eighth grade. Back then it wasn't about talent shows as much as it was about battling on the playground during recess. We would huddle in a group that would gradually expand as other people figured out what was going on. There was normally a neutral, respected beatboxer kicking the beat for all of the emcees, and we would stand toe-to-toe working either from memory or going completely off the dome. Some days you'd win; some days you'd lose. At nights, you'd just go back to your notebook and write some more rhymes, memorize them, get out on the playground the next day, and battle your ass off.

I did this all the way through high school, and when I went to college, I found a few other emcees and we would cipher deep into the night. I even thought a record deal might come out of all of it, but it never turned out that way. Instead, I parlayed my love of poetry into a thesis on the Harlem Renaissance and then a dissertation on Langston Hughes.

Now here I was in my home office with a notepad stretched out in front of me nodding to a Kanye West instrumental, earbuds sealed tightly in my ears. I didn't even notice my little girl walk up beside me with a small gift-wrapped box in her hands. I yanked the buds out of my ears and said, "Thank you, sweetie." I looked back and saw my wife standing in the doorway smiling.

"Open it, Daddy," Lena said, unable conceal her own smile.

I undid the package as carefully as I could while my daughter and wife waited patiently. When I lifted the lid on the box and saw a book that read *Rhyming Dictionary* inside, I grabbed my daughter and hugged her tightly. "Thank you, sweetie," I said.

I stood and walked over to my wife and gave her the kind of kiss that I normally reserved for her when we were in our bedroom.

"Ooooooh," Lena said. "Mommy and Daddy sittin' in a tree K-I-S-S-I-N-G!"

We turned to face our daughter and smiled sheepishly. Lena covered her mouth, giggling, but I could tell that she was happy to see her parents being romantic.

When they left me alone in the room with my new reference tool, I felt much better about the coming weekend. I had never used a rhyming dictionary, but the fact that my family had my back was far more important than any two words I could have strung together in verse.

On Saturday morning I hopped in the shower freestyling about anything I could think of, most of it just flat-out ridiculous. I even rhymed about the Axe shower gel I was using. Anything I could rhyme, I rhymed. By the time I finished breakfast with my family, I started getting ideas about what it was like growing up on the streets of Memphis and pushing myself to go to college at FAMU on scholarship just to get away from home. I grabbed my notepad and started jotting down ideas. Some of it was good, and some of it was definitely headed for the cutting room floor.

Throughout the day I tweaked my lyrics over and over until I thought I had something flexible enough for whatever beat Noble was going to throw at me. I quickly realized that my delivery style was a mixture of animation and seriousness, and I worried I would just sound like an old dude trying too hard. So I took my smartphone and started recording myself saying the words, trying different inflections and intonations. Every time I played back my sixteen bars, I flinched. I wasn't cut out for this. They would surely laugh at me and probably take me off the track altogether.

It seemed as if the more I practiced my rap, the worse I sounded, until finally I just took the sheet of paper and crumbled it up and threw it in the trash. Rather than waste any more time on this nonsense, I was going to go and see what was on cable. No sooner than I popped the leg rest on the recliner did my wife walk into the room.

"What are you doing?" she asked.

"I'm done. I can't do this anymore. I'm just not cut out for this. I'm not trying to play myself with these kids."

I could see the space between her eyebrows furrow, and I knew immediately that she didn't agree with my assessment. "But you've been working so hard."

"Baby, I'm thirty-eight. I have no business trying to bust a rhyme. I don't even sound right rapping. I sound like an Oreo," I said.

"A what?"

"An Oreo: black on the outside and white on the inside."

She shook her head. "No you don't. You sound like an intelligent, strong Black man," she said.

I smiled. "I know what you're doing. You're trying to do that Regina King/Cuba Gooding, Jr. thing on me from *Jerry Maguire*."

She chuckled softly before responding, "I love you, so I'm going to tell you the truth. If you were some wack brother, I wouldn't be with you."

I shrugged, picking the remote control back up off of the end table. "I could do a lot less damage just staying here today."

She walked over and stood between me and the television. "What made you say yes to this kid in the first place?"

I sighed. "I just wanted to show everyone that I still had it."

"And you don't want to do that any more?" she asked.

"No," I said, putting the remote control down.

"I don't blame you."

"So then we agree?" I said.

My wife shook her head. "No, actually we don't. The difference between you and me is that you think you should do this for other people, and I think you should do it for yourself."

I couldn't find the words to respond to her comment. Instead I sat there replaying her words in my mind. That's when Lena walked into the room singing Willow Smith's song "Whip My Hair."

My wife looked at me and then at our daughter. I turned off the television and looked down at my watch. It was three o'clock. Clearly I had to get myself ready for my appointment at five.

In the drive over to the studio, I steadied my breath and cleared my head. My lyrics were in the garbage can back at home. I would be freestyling my sixteen bars today, and while I had no idea of how I wanted to start or end, whether I wanted to use metaphors or personification or any word play with homophones, I knew I was going to say whatever was on my heart. I remembered what it was like to stand in the battle huddles in junior high, what it felt like to be sitting in the dorm kicking sixteen bars around the cipher circle at two in the morning, what it felt like to hear a J. Dilla track for the first time, and what it felt like to hear The Legendary Roots Crew rock a crowd in a small Philly club.

When I walked through the door of the studio, Noble dapped me and introduced me around.

"You ready?" he asked.

"About as ready as I'll ever be," I responded.

He showed me to the recording booth, and I put on the headphones that were wrapped around the microphone stand.

"We'll play the track a few times for you, and you can see how your lyrics fit with the beat before we record."

"Okay," I said, as the engineer turned on the music in my headphones. I could feel the beat moving in my chest, the bassline expanding in my head. I couldn't place the track, but I could tell the sample was from Earth, Wind & Fire. I closed my eyes and cleared my head. After a minute, I said, "I'm ready."

Noble said, "Word? You write your stuff down?"

"No, I'm going off the dome."

"That's what's up," he said, nodding his head.

We did a mic check to make sure the levels were right and that my voice was picking up properly, and then Noble left for the engineering booth.

Alone in the recording booth for the first time, the beat still moving through my head, I smiled. I was actually here—after all of this time. This was what I had always wanted. This was my chance to put a creative piece of myself into existence.

I could hear Noble in my headset. "We're about to drop the beat. Just come in when you're ready."

My mind was as clear as the waters of the Caribbean. I inhaled, the beat enveloping me like the embrace of a long-lost lover. The bassline moved like a jump rope being swung widely in an arc, inviting me.

I leaned forward, opened my mouth, and jumped in.

* *This story originally appeared in* Bessie, Bop, or Bach: Collected Stories *by Ran Walker.*

AUTHOR'S NOTE

This book contains references to premature birth. In 2019, doctors and nurses are able to do a great deal more to increase the chances of survival and development for premature babies. This does not happen, however, without the work of organizations like the March of Dimes.

My family supports this organization, and if you are interested in donating to help the March of Dimes continue their work in this area, you may do so at www.marchofdimes.org.

Thank you in advance for your consideration.

ACKNOWLEDGMENTS

I would like to thank my boy Sabin Prentis for his constant support of this project. I'd also like to thank Tayari Jones, my good friend and mentor, for her encouragement.

A special thank you goes out to Phonte Coleman, whose song "Tigallo for Dolo" helped to inspire this work.

Thank you to my brother, Torrey, who continues to motivate and inspire me; my father, who encourages me regularly; and my mother, who turned me on to my love of books.

Last, but by no means least, I would like to thank my wife, Lauren, for her patience, love, and support; and my daughter, Zoë, who makes me the proudest father in the world.

ALSO BY RAN WALKER

B-Sides and Remixes
30 Love: A Novel
Mojo's Guitar: A Novel/(Il était une fois Morris Jones)
Afro Nerd in Love: A Novella
The Keys of My Soul: A Novel
The Race of Races: A Novel
The Illest: A Novella
Bessie, Bop, or Bach: Collected Stories
Four Floors (with Sabin Prentis)
Black Hand Side: Stories
White Pages: A Novel
She Lives in My Lap
Reverb
Work-In-Progress
Daykeeper
Most of My Heroes Don't Appear On No Stamps
Portable Black Magic

ABOUT THE AUTHOR

Ran Walker is the award-winning author of seventeen books. His work has appeared in a variety of anthologies and journals. He and his family live in Virginia, where he works as a creative writing professor at Hampton University.

www.ingramcontent.com/pod-product-compliance
Lightning Source LLC
Chambersburg PA
CBHW070431010526
44118CB00014B/1998